How To Double Your Sales
Without
Quadrupling Your Effort

Jim Meisenheimer

A Helbern Book

Helbern
Published by the Helbern Group
Libertyville, Illinois 60048, U.S.A.

Helbern Group, Registered Offices:
824 Paddock Lane, Libertyville, Illinois

Second Helbern Printing, October 2003
10 9 8 7 6 5 4 3 2

Printed in the United States of America

Library of Congress Catalogue Card Number: 98-094065

ISBN 0-9637479-2-4

For
Helen, Eileen and Rudy

Thanks for all your love and encouragement.

Contents

Introduction

The Predicament:
What's Holding You Back?

Part I

Double Your Sales By
Developing An "ATTITUDE"

i

Part II

Get A Grip On Your Life
Don't Quadruple Your Effort

Part III

Win More Sales
By Acting Like A Pro

Introduction

The Predicament:
What's Holding You Back?

"Make everyday a masterpiece," that's what I tell salespeople. The best way to accomplish this is to always start with your customers not with your products. In preparing to write this book, I took my own advice. I started with my customers - salespeople. I know all salespeople want to sell more, but I wasn't sure what was holding them back from achieving success.

So I created a survey that asked salespeople to evaluate sixteen situations or challenges. The results include data from over seventy companies and thirteen hundred salespeople.

The results of the survey surprised me. The top five challenges had little to do with selling. I was expecting salespeople to say "dealing with demanding customers, handling the price objection, and getting to the decision-maker" would be the biggest challenges.

Take the survey to see if your responses match the ones I've collected.

My biggest challenges . . . Sales Survey

Listed below are sixteen challenges and situations encountered by professional salespeople. Score each item using a scale from 1 to 10, with a 1 meaning it's "no challenge," and a 10 representing "one of my biggest challenges."

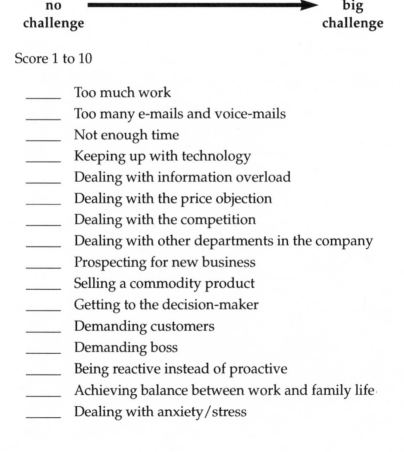

1 2 3 4 5 6 7 8 9 10

no challenge ⟶ big challenge

Score 1 to 10

_____ Too much work
_____ Too many e-mails and voice-mails
_____ Not enough time
_____ Keeping up with technology
_____ Dealing with information overload
_____ Dealing with the price objection
_____ Dealing with the competition
_____ Dealing with other departments in the company
_____ Prospecting for new business
_____ Selling a commodity product
_____ Getting to the decision-maker
_____ Demanding customers
_____ Demanding boss
_____ Being reactive instead of proactive
_____ Achieving balance between work and family life
_____ Dealing with anxiety/stress

How To Double Your Sales Without Quadrupling Your Effort

According to the survey, salespeople needed advice on how to get rid of time busters, how to achieve balance in their professional and personal lives, and how to focus on achieving maximum results in minimum time.

The prioritized results of the survey were:

#1 Not enough time
#2 Achieving balance between work and family life
#3 Dealing with information overload
#4 Too much work
#5 Dealing with anxiety/stress
#6 Dealing with the competition
#7 Being reactive instead of proactive
#8 Dealing with the price objection
#9 Keeping up with technology
#10 Prospecting for new business
#11 Dealing with other departments in the company
#12 Demanding customers
#13 Getting to the decision-maker
#14 Too many e-mails and voice-mails
#15 Selling a commodity product
#16 Demanding boss

Part I

Doubling Your Sales by Developing An "ATTITUDE"

1. "A" - Aim: Aim Higher

The purpose of aiming at a target is to achieve results. As an archer draws his arrow from his quiver, his sight and thoughts are focused on the center of the target. Adjustments are made for distance and wind. If the archer could never hit the bull's-eye, why would he keeping aiming at it? The archer aims because he's rewarded, if his skills are good, with the prize called bull's-eye.

In sales, the targets are different. They aren't the paper targets deer hunters use to sharpen their skills. The targets are numbers. Often these numbers are expressed in sales dollars and gross profit dollars. Sometimes the targets or quotas, as they are more commonly referred to, are expressed in tons or units. These quotas can also be assigned as percentages of profitability and sales increases.

I have never met a salesperson who finished the year at exactly 100.00% of an assigned quota. It just never happens. What does happen is that the salesperson may finish the year with a 98.2% achievement, just missing the target. Sometimes

1

a sales representative, may finish with a 101.1% achievement to plan, barely exceeding his target. Still other times salespeople may finish either substantially higher or lower than their annual target.

Review your own performance numbers for as long as you've been selling. Just remember, no rounding up is permitted, in this instance. How many times have you missed the target? If hitting the bull's-eye in sales is virtually impossible, why are you aiming for it?

Forget about every future sales quota you are given. That's your company's number. Now I'm not anti-company numbers at all. Your company must give you a number or quota to shoot for. All the numbers within a company are added together to create the annual sales forecast. A company without a forecast won't ever get to be leader of the pack. They'll probably end up being the dog of your industry.

Aiming for the company number isn't where the action really is. Here's my recommendation. Take whatever quota you're given and add something to it. It doesn't have to be a lot. It could be 2.0% more. It could be 1.75% more. By adjusting your aim higher and internalizing your revised number, it will have a positive impact on your performance. Look at it this way. How could aiming higher have a negative impact on your selling results?

Adjusting your aim at the start of your fiscal year has all the benefits and no down sides. You'll always achieve greater results. You'll always earn a larger income. If you want to achieve more don't settle for the company's quota. It's all about aiming higher.

2. "T" - Tango: Learn to dance with your customers

Last January I was scheduled to deliver the keynote speech for a security company's annual management conference. Since the meeting was going to be at the Sheraton Universal in Universal City, California I flew into LAX airport.

I had my luggage with me, so I was able to by-pass baggage claim. It was late, about 9:00 PM, when I approached the taxi stand. There were four cabs in line and no passengers in sight. I walked to the first taxi in line.

The driver opened his door and hurried out to greet me. He quickly took my bag from me and placed it into his trunk. Once seated, the taxi started for the exit, the driver turned around and said, "We're off to Las Vegas." Well, I was half asleep; when I realized what he'd said, I shouted, "No, I'm not going to Las Vegas, I want to go to Universal City." He smiled when he said, "Just joking."

After a few minutes on the freeway, he asked me if I wanted to listen to any particular kind of music. I told him the channel he had on was fine. It was nice that he asked though. His taxi, I began to notice, was immaculate. Today you seldom find really clean taxicabs.

A short while later he asked what brought me from Chicago to California (he had checked my luggage tags). I told him about my morning presentation. He showed a genuine interest in

3

my work. The driver indicated that he had been to a couple of seminars since he arrived from the Philippines. He said he believed in education, though his priority was to save so he could bring his family over from the Philippines to join him. He talked a little about his family and I talked a little about mine.

As we pulled up to the hotel, I began thinking that this had been a very pleasant taxi experience because of the driver. I asked if he would be interested in taking me back to the airport tomorrow at 11:00 AM. He responded enthusiastically. He offered a receipt, completely filled out, and removed my suitcase from the trunk.

He handed me my bag and I paid him including a generous tip. He smiled and then reached over and shook my hand and said, "Thank you very much." It's the first time in thirty-three years of taking cabs that the driver shook my hand and said "Thank you."

His name was William Wee. I included him in my presentation the following morning as an example of outstanding customer service. At 11:00 AM, as I walked out the front door of the hotel, I spotted William buffing the outside of his already immaculate taxi. When he saw me, he smiled and waved and rushed over to get my bag. After saying hello, he asked how my presentation went. I told him that I had told the group about his excellent customer service. He was very happy to hear that.

William shakes my hand and I get a lesson in customer service. Wow!

Ask most cab drivers, what makes them different and they'll tell you how long they have been driving and how they know all the short cuts. Ask William Wee the same question and you'll get a different answer. William is totally focused on his customers. What makes him different is his obsession to provide the best taxi service in Los Angeles.

Elbow-grease is the best polish.

English Proverb

Action is eloquence.

Shakespeare

Getting people to like you is merely the other side of liking them.

Norman Vincent Peale

5

3. "T" - Tenacity: Develop velcro-like stick-to-it-tiveness

Tenacity means everything to success in selling. It means being determined, resolute, purposeful and having the will to persevere. How often is success determined by an extra step, incremental effort or the mind set to do something extra? Focusing on the objective, and being patient enough to persist, is not for the weak-spirited nor the typical run-of-the-mill salesperson. What separates the real winners from the rest of the pack is tenacity. Here are some very special thoughts from some very tenacious people.

It's not whether you get knocked down, it's whether you get up.

Vince Lombardi

My attitude has always been . . . if it's worth playing, it's worth paying the price to win.

Bear Bryannt

The rung of a ladder was never meant to rest upon, but only to hold a man's foot long enough to enable him to put the other somewhat higher.

Thomas Huxley

The difficult we do immediately; the impossible takes a little longer.

> Air Force Motto

Great things are done when men and mountains meet.

> William Blake

God is with those who persevere.

> The Koran

Most people give up just when they're about to achieve success, they give up at the last minute of the game, one foot from a winning touchdown.

> H. Ross Perot

To succeed, we must have the will to succeed, we must have stamina, determination, backbone, perseverance, self-reliance, and faith.

> B.C. Forbes

When the truly great people discover that they have been deceived by the signposts along the road of life, they just shift gears and keep on going.

> Nido Qubein

The person who makes a success of living is the one who sees his goal steadily and aims for it unswervingly. That is dedication.

> Cecil B. De Mille

*Stopping at third base adds no more to the score
than striking out.*

Anonymous

*The road to success runs uphill, so don't expect to
break any speed records.*

Anonymous

*The basic rules for success may be defined as follows:
Know what you want. Find out what it takes to get
it. Act on it and persevere.*

Anonymous

*The secret to success is to start from scratch and
keep on scratching.*

Anonymous

Most of us have what it takes to be really successful, we simply forget to apply it. No one is shut out of the tenacity department. At times, you have experienced the results of personal tenacity and have savored success. Think about a time when you achieved success, especially when it required a great deal of effort and perseverance. Take a few minutes to write it down in your new insights journal - a composition notebook where you record new ideas and successes. If you've been successful before, there's no reason you can't repeat your success. It's one thing to be inspired by the words and deeds of the "Great Ones," it's more meaningful to be inspired by your accomplishments.

Next time you consider giving up or tossing in the towel, review your notes for inspiration. Tenacity is like a vine; once planted it continues to grow.

4. "I" - Impact: Style vs. substance

It's the classic debate. Which is more important, style or substance? Usually, the advocates in the debate favor and emphasize their own strengths. According to author Leslie Smith, "Style is not the enemy of substance, and only people with lousy self-images tend to think otherwise."

According to Smith, the word "style" comes from the Latin "stylus," which described the metal pencil used to write with on a wax tablet and, metaphorically, the personal characteristics of a person's writing. Style is individual and should be distinctive.

We all make personal judgments based on style. Put yourself in this situation. You're attending a national sales conference. The newly hired vice-president of sales walks into the meeting room. You've seen his photograph so you know it's him. At first glance he strikes you as authoritative and poised. He seems to be in control and assertive. Your first impression includes a sense that he is direct and to the point and very action oriented. He also appears to be likable and approachable.

Mind you, all these impressions, were formed at a distance of fifteen feet. Up to this point you haven't been introduced or heard him say a word. So, what influenced and created these first impressions?

Jim Meisenheimer

Lord Chesterfield once wrote, "Dress is a foolish thing, and yet it is a foolish thing not to be well-dressed." The navy blue suit the vice-president was wearing made a statement. So did the handsomely designed, bold and powerful red tie. His shirt was a crisp white. As he approached, you couldn't help but be impressed with his shoes, obviously polished for the occasion.

Bolstering his appearance was the way he carried himself. The first thing you noticed was his chin angled up. Then there was the bounce to his walk, a confident stride. As he approached people to introduce himself, his hand glided out to initiate the greeting and introductions. All of this, plus a broad and genuine smile.

Sherlock Holmes, a fictional great, once remarked, "It has long been an axiom of mine that the little things are infinitely the most important."

Even before we say something, many people have formed lasting opinions about us. We live in visually acute and sensitive times. We are surrounded by videos and global netscapes. What people see says a lot about you. How you look conveys who you are. Style without substance is a charade. Substance without style is unforgivable.

5. "T" - Think: Become a sales strategist

Learn to think before you react. There are two principal activities in selling. One is reactive and the other is proactive. The former is a responder and the latter is an initiator. Analyze your "To Do List" for last week. How much time was spent responding to phone calls, E-mails, voice mails, customer requests and management demands. Avoid the "pity me syndrome" rationalizing you had no choice but to respond to all the demands on your time.

You're either reactive or proactive. The difference rests in your ability to prioritize. Darting from contact to contact within a large account may represent hard work, but is it smart work? Selling products before you understand needs seldom works, and when it does work it invariably consumes more time. Arriving at the prospect's doorstep without a written call plan becomes evident quickly. Rambling presentations that miss the targeted opportunity don't motivate potential customers to buy.

People are desperately searching for solutions to their very unique problems. Lead with your questions, not with your products. Start with your customers never with your services. Do your homework before you take the exam. This is practical advice for achieving selling success. Take the advice and you'll win more business. Ignore it and you'll suffer the consequences.

11

What should you plan and when should you plan? First plan every call. Planning a sales call is a simple process. Your call plan should answer the question: "What's the specific purpose of this sales call?" The key words are "specific purpose." Your objectives must be quantifiable to be really effective. If they are quantifiable, they include numbers. An example is, "The purpose of this call is to secure another meeting with the decision-makers within two weeks." Having the number "two" in your objective, makes the objective very specific. When your objective is specific, your focus becomes more narrow, and that's what you want.

Plan all your calls the night before you make them. A call that's planned in advance, is a call that can be changed if necessary. Unplanned sales calls rarely make the buyer's day. Imagine a potential customer saying, "You were so disorganized today, that I really enjoyed talking with you."

Once you have a call plan, it's time to consider an account plan. First do your homework. Ask a dozen really provocative questions before you even think about planning how you'll secure the business. Ideally, you'll want to begin building your account plan after you've done your homework and before you start presenting solutions. This approach favors a longer than average selling cycle. Most large sales aren't hatched in one or even two sales calls. There are three elements to a really good and well written account plan: goals, strategies and tactics.

First, determine what your specific goals for your account are. Be sure your goals include product mix, sales dollars and target completion dates. Your goals are "what" you want to achieve. The clearer your goals, the higher the probability of making a sale. For example, "My goal is to sell seven different products at 40% profit and have all orders in house by June 6, 2001."

Second, once you mapped out in writing "what" you want to sell, determine "how" you'll do the "what's". The strategies are a series of how's. The stronger the how's the better your chances. Don't be stingy with your how's. Make sure you've considered all your options. If there is ever a time to turn on your creative juices, it is now as you start to think about your strategies. Few strategies are strategic enough to be called strategic. Ask yourself this question. "What's the probability I'll succeed, if I implement all my strategies?" If you don't foresee at least a 75% probability, revisit your personal think-tank. Your strategies are the glue that holds the your plan together.

Third, remember every strategy has details to be taken care of. Tactics are details. Don't get blind-sided by sloppy work or rushed agendas. To take care of all the details, you must wear your analytical hat temporarily, regardless of how uncomfortable it feels. Something as common as an entertainment strategy for a large prospect includes many details. For example: Who should be asked to attend the dinner? What kind of food does your decision-maker prefer? Who will make the reservations? Who will invite the clients? Who will invite members of your team? Where and when will you meet? Who will pick up the tab? How will you be seated, especially if it's a large group? Who will send thank you notes? Will there be a recap meeting to review the results? Who will attend, etc., etc.

Selling can be fun. Planning can be boring and tedious. Getting the order as a result of a carefully executed plan can be a huge thrill because, not only did you do it, you had the whole thing planned.

Planning your sale and selling your plan is a secret to success that few salespeople ever master. The journey to success is paved with well executed plans.

Make haste slowly.

Augustus

Imagination is more important than knowledge.

Albert Einstein

Genius begins great works; labor alone finishes them.

Joubert

6. "U" Upside down: To change or not to change

Conventional thinking is out. Unconventional thinking is in, or should be. Our world is shrinking; technology is exploding; consolidation is running wild; and nearly everything is disposable. The best salespeople are rearranging the deck chairs on the ship of selling.

Improvement is everywhere. Make changes or bite the dust. Be responsive or lose your competitive advantage. The message for salespeople is simple; get a grip, get a life, and get ready to make some changes in the way you approach the business of selling. The process of self-improvement is like the distant horizon, we walk toward it and never quite reach it.

Here are the three most important steps in the selling process. They are traditional steps. Your challenge is to rethink, reexamine and rework them to fit today's demanding customer base. Ask this question for each of the steps - "Is there a better way to do it?"

Networking
"Networking" is one letter away from "not working". Networking is the acquired skill of reaching out to connect with the multitudes. Too many salespeople have too few names on their business Rolodex. Most salespeople don't even now how many names are on their Rolodex. If there is something more important than your business network, I'd

15

love to know what it is. Here are three gottas. You gotta know how many contacts are on your Rolodex. You gotta do something to stay connected with the names on your list. You also gotta creatively figure out how to expand your network.

Asking the right questions
What's your favorite open-ended question you rely on to discover customer needs? If you have to think about it, you aren't where you need to be in the questioning process. A salesperson without questions is like a comedian without jokes. It's not funny. Forget everything you know about questions. Prepare a list of things you'd like to know about potential customers. Prioritize the list. Arrange the list in a logical sequence. Once you've done this, prepare a question for each. Make certain the question can't be answered in one or two words.

Listening carefully
Listening is activated by closing your mouth. Talking doesn't help you learn. Listening does. There are three things you can do to jump-start your listening skills, no matter how poorly you currently listen. First, you should ask really good questions. A question is like a match to a fire, it gets the conversation going. Asking good questions is the number one priority for effective listening. The number two priority is to take notes after you ask your question. When you take notes you are telegraphing to your potential customer that what he just said was noteworthy. Lastly, put quotes in your notes. Any time your potential customer says something colorful, provoking, or even spicy, be sure you capture it and wrap quotes around it. There is no better way to relate to a person than by using his own words in your conversation.

7. "D" - Different: To be better you gotta be different

Do you think you're above average? Most people do. Lake Wobegone was a fictitious area named by author Garrison Keillor where "all the women are strong, all the men are good looking, and all the children are above average." In his book, *Selling The Invisible*, author Harry Beckwith, describes the "Effect" as overestimating yourself. He cites a survey where 60% of the students questioned ranked themselves in the top 10% in their ability to get along.

When salespeople overestimate their skills and abilities they place themselves at a competitive disadvantage. No where is this more evident than in the seminars I present. Picture this as the setting. Twenty-five sales representatives are seated at tables of five. Ninety minutes into the program, I ask them to list and discuss several specific things that differentiate them from competitive salespeople they know. In creating their lists, they are instructed not to differentiate their products or their companies.

The results are always consistent and very predictable. To make the point, as they are writing their lists, I turn a flip chart around and write down what I'm anticipating they will include on their lists. It never fails; the lists match. What's even more astonishing is that the lists are always the same. To the question, "What makes you different from competitive salespeople?" the responses include: integrity, product knowledge, work experience, adaptability, responsiveness, loyalty, sincerity, caring, customer follow-ups, timely visits, etc.

These are admirable qualities. They don't, however, differentiate the playing field. Salespeople are consumed by the influence of assumptions and generalities. There appears to be an inborn tendency to believe that competitors don't measure up in the integrity department, have less experience and knowledge, and just basically don't treat their customers very well.

There are three principle things you can differentiate when selling: you, your products, and your company. My observation is that most sales reps do an adequate job of differentiating their products and their company. They neglect, however, to develop their personal trademarks. Before a customer considers buying your product, they gotta buy you. The real difference between salespeople is what's inside their heads - their ideas. To offer generalities when the customers are begging for specificity misses the mark. Don't ever permit generalities to obscure the real differences between you and your competitors.

"Wow! Now that was a professional sales representative." Wouldn't you love to hear your potential customers whispering those words as you're leaving the account? Being boring, bland and benign won't cut it. If you want to make a difference you gotta be different. Let me give you some examples.

Captain Dennis C. Schaar
There are nine thousand pilots with United Airlines. Imagine if we could line them up and ask each one what makes them

different from other pilots? Most would describe their total flying hours, some would describe in detail all the different planes they've flown, still others would boast of their military experience. Nothing different about that.

When you're flying first class with United, as a guest on Captain Dennis C. Schaar's flight, you'll experience a real touch of class. As an Executive Premier Gold Card holder with United Airlines, I upgrade to first class approximately 85% of the time. Last January, I flew from Chicago to Charlotte, North Carolina. In command on the flight deck, as they like to say, was Captain Dennis Schaar.

Ten minutes before the wheels touched down, our flight attendant gave cards to all passengers in first class. It was a business card. The face of the card included Captain Dennis C. Schaar's name and home address with phone number. Also on the card was the United Airlines logo. On the reverse, the card was dated, had my name, and the following short note.

Thank you for flying with us today.
Your business is truly appreciated.

Regards,
Dennis

It's not a big thing. Actually it's quite a small thing. Size however has little to do with the point. It's different, and few pilots do it. Captain Schaar has differentiated himself from

from tens of thousands of airline pilots with his handwritten notes making everyone in first class feel special on his flights. It doesn't have to be big to feel good. Unlike most pilots, Captain Schaar realizes the people in First Class, are the most frequent flyers. His little notes keep bringing us back.

Dr. Nick Polito

> Roses are red, violets are blue,
> have you been thinking about
> your dentist, because we've
> been thinking about you?

The small card was signed - "Dr. Nick, Denise, Gail, Margaret, Kelly, and Roberta." I came home after a two-day sales training trip in California and found on the kitchen table a straw basket filled with cookies, candies, coffee packets and three helium balloons that said "We miss you." I must confess, I initially thought the basket was for me from Bernadette, my wife.

After a little teasing and some ribbing, she showed me the card. Here's a good dentist with a sense of humor creatively reminding my wife that she's due for a checkup. It sure beats the post cards most of us get.

On a different occasion, when I had the pleasure of being seated in Dr. Nick's examination chair, I asked him what his priorities were for his practice. He took a moment to think, before he spoke. Dr. Nick said providing "exceptional dentistry" was his number one priority. I guess most dentists, if asked, wouldn't say "exceptional dentistry" is their top priority. Then again, most dentists wouldn't send you a basket of goodies and balloons to remind you it's time for a visit.

Going to the dentist is not something to look forward to, going to see Dr. Nick is. You don't think about pain as much. You think about fun and a caring person who happens to be a dentist.

Chris Clarke Epstein
Chris Clarke Epstein is a fellow professional speaker. She likes to send Christmas cards in February. Here's what her card said.

> I really thought I had learned my lesson last year because it was so embarrassing sending holiday greetings in February. I had all the good intentions in the world to never let that happen again until, that is November flew by with meetings right up to Thanksgiving and people who are far more organized than I am started sending cards that arrived with increasing frequency on my desk reminding me that I was running behind again and if I didn't do something really soon I'd be right where I was last year. As I turned the page in my Franklin Planner to the beginning of December I resolved to get right on it and I started thinking about all I wanted to say because it's really important to me to find the right words to express my deep feelings of gratitude and appreciation for the wonderful people who are part of my work and life. But finding the

perfect words to say a sincere thank you for your friendship and business takes a long time so here we are in January (which is better than February) and I'm late again but still sincere in wishing you all the best from January 1996 to January 1997!

Like you, I get a lot of Christmas cards. I can only remember one card because it got my attention and was really different. That card stood out like the Lone Ranger in my mail the day I received it. I still have it. Being different doesn't take money, it takes imagination and time.

It's easy to do what everyone else does. Copycats aren't differentiated and therefore seldom get rewarded. Originality is its own reward. If you want to be remembered do something memorable. Be like Chris.

The Ship's Inn, Exton, Pennsylvania

We went to The Ship's Inn, in Exton Pennsylvania the night before a scheduled sales training program, because the director of sales invited me to dinner. It was a windy, blustery, rainy winter's night. The restaurant was in what was formerly a large home. At the entrance there was a center hallway with a spiral staircase leading to the second floor. There were two small dining rooms, one to the left and the other to the right. We were seated in the room to the left. It used to be the living room and had a fine looking stone fireplace that was fired up with several huge oak logs.

What can I say, the place was great. The service was good and the food left little to be desired. My host wanted to discuss the training program which we did throughout the dinner. As we finished dinner, the waiter approached and asked "Would you like me to clear your plates to make more room on the table for you?" Over the years I've had the opportunity to eat at a number of restaurants. Lots of waiters have removed plates, but none said it the way he did. We glanced at each other and then looked at the waiter. I was impressed and asked him where he learned those words. He said he was trained at the Culinary Institute. We chatted for a few minutes and learned a little about his training. The meal was good and he made it even better. In restaurants, good service gets rewarded - the customers keep coming back. The waiter providing the service also gets rewarded. Saying the right thing is usually more dependent on preparation than improvisation.

That night our waiter received a very generous tip and here's a tip for you . . . remember, when you're different it really makes a difference.

To get you started in the right direction, I'd like to share three ideas that may add to your personal trademark. This trademark will identify you as a salesperson with a unique selling style.

The three ideas have one thing in common, they are all cards. The first card is the easiest to send, if you remember to do it. Whenever you go away on vacation, always bring a supply of postage stamps. It's practically impossible to go a vacation without visiting a gift shop. All gift shops sell post cards featuring your vacation destination. Here's the concept. Buy twenty postcards. Send ten to your best customers and the other ten to your biggest prospects. A short note is all you need. The card says you care. The card says you cared enough to write a note to your customers and prospects even when you're away on vacation.

The second idea is to send a special occasion business card. For example, one of your potential customers isn't returning your calls. How about a card that has a photo of a basketball, laying on the floor.

The ball's in your court!

Open the card and the words "The ball's in your court!" appear over your business card.

When your potential customer is considering you and your competitor's product, think of sending him a card with a photo of an apple and an orange placed over the word "comparisons." Inside your prospect sees these words, "The most fruitful decisions . . . rely on accurate comparisons. I'd like to provide you with information to help you in your decision making process." Once again these words appear above your business card.

To stay connected with your customers consider sending a card that shows a collection of timepieces and the words "Time flies!"

It's been a while since we've spoken.
Let's talk soon.

Inside the inscription reads, "It's been a while since we've spoken. Let's talk soon." These cards and others like them are available from Introknocks. Call them for a catalog. (800) 753-0590.

The third idea and it may very well be the most potent card you can send is an anniversary card. The impact is equally high for customers and potential customers. I have discovered that all people employed share a common characteristic. Everybody remembers and can easily recall the month and the year they started working for a company. For example, you are calling on someone who works for a large pharmaceutical company. Ask the person how long they have worked in the pharmaceutical industry. He'll usually respond with the number of years he's been working in that industry. Follow up and ask him which month of that year he began working. Everybody remembers the month and the year they got started, don't you?

Now, all you have to do is to remember to send a card to that person. Here's how it works. Once you obtain the information, you should enter it in your account management or data base management software program. Both generally include calenders with pop up reminders. Enter the information into your software, which should allow you to make the reminder recurring on an annual basis. The first of every month you'll be reminded to send specific cards to the people with anniversaries that month.

Think about this - everybody remembers the month and the year they started working at a particular job or in a special field. If that's true, then it must be important. What's paradoxical about this is only one person knows and remembers the date and that's the person we're talking to. Do your family and friends send you cards every year acknowledging your anniversary? Probably not; that's what makes an anniversary card a very special card. Using the above as an example, a short note saying, "Congratulations on your 17th year as a buyer in the pharmaceutical industry" would remind the recipient of your thoughtfulness year after year.

One final thought on cards. You must write them before you send them. If you're going to start writing cards regularly, buy a fountain pen. We live in high tech times and the fountain pen screams high touch. It's another example of how you can be different.

Being different requires curiosity, creativity, and commitment. It takes curiosity to seek better ways of doing things. Imagine your favorite question is, "Is there a better way?" Also imagine applying that question to the subject of differentiation. Once you ask the question, "Is there a better way?" your creativity kicks in and takes over. Don't underestimate your creativity potential. You don't need the title of Creative Director to be creative. It takes commitment to make it work. Most salespeople aren't committed to being different and it shows. Those that do focus on differentiation are recognized, remembered and rewarded for their efforts.

When we are overly smitten with our abilities, we rarely take the time to sharpen our edge. A blade that's not sharpened, becomes dull. This is a perilous strategy, at a time when customers are more demanding, competition is intense, and technology is radically changing how we sell. It's wiser to assume you're inferior to the competition and begin searching for ways to differentiate and distance yourself from them in the future.

Jim Meisenheimer

If you begin with the premise that you're average, you'll end with results that aren't.

> *The best things are the most difficult.*
> > Greek Proverb

> *Men are born equal but they are also born different.*
> > Erich Fromm

> *Anybody who is any good is different from anybody else.*
> > Felix Frankfurter

8. "E" - Exuders: It's show time

The attitude factor plays a huge role in determining selling success. Attitude can be defined many ways, but I believe attitude has two major components: how you feel and what you exude. It's really two dimensional. It starts with how you feel and what you're thinking. For you it's internalized. When you're interacting with other people, especially when salespeople are calling on customers, what you feel is what the customer observes. You are exuding stuff. It's either good stuff or it's bad stuff.

It's critical for a professional sales representative to project an upbeat, enthusiastic, and positive attitude on each and every sales call. That of course is easy to say and hard to execute for some salespeople, because of the human factor. Four years ago I was conducting a two-day selling skills seminar for a Canadian health care company. The session was being held in a beautiful winter ski resort located in Deerhurst, about two hours north of Toronto.

There were fifty-five salespeople and managers participating in the program. The momentum up to the point I'm going to describe was extremely positive. The subject on the afternoon of the second day was attitude. I was describing how important it is for salespeople to always project a positive attitude throughout a sales call. A woman raised her hand.

She said:

> Jim, I've been listening to everything you've
> said and by the way have agreed with most of
> it, but this attitude crap is nothing but
> nonsense. Look, if I'm having a good day
> you'll know it, and if for any reason I'm not
> you'll also know that. I don't believe in faking
> something as important as that.

Well, there goes the class, it was like a wave in full motion.
First I had them and then as they listened to her words, heads
began nodding and other people wanted to add their
comments to support her. I couldn't let that happen, because I
truly believe that your attitude must be positive on every sales
call and there are no exceptions.

So, here's what I did. I suggested a hypothetical situation. I
told her that I certainly didn't wish this on her, but let's
pretend that tomorrow you are scheduled for serious brain
surgery. At 8:00 AM your surgeon and anesthesiologist walk
into your room. The surgeon approaches your bed, asks how
you're doing. The patient looks up at the doctor and says
she's a little nervous. She asks how the doctor is doing and he
replies, "Don't ask, I've had better days. This morning my car
was totaled. I realize, I should be thankful because I wasn't in
the car, but it's still on my mind."

I asked the woman, in that set of circumstances how she
would feel about having surgery under those circumstances.
She did acknowledge that it wouldn't make her feel very
comfortable. I asked her about her expectations for the
surgery and the surgeon. She described high expectations.

She didn't care to know what personal problems he was dealing with. She wanted him to be focused on her and her operation. In this case the attitude of the surgeon is critically important. The proper mental attitude is also very important on every sales call. There never has been and never will be a substitute for a great attitude.

If you're going to expect others to adjust their attitudes for you, make sure yours is properly aligned to the situation you're in. The quickest way to adjust your attitude is to periodically check a small mirror. This is usually easier for women than men, but the advice should be followed by both. A mirror keeps your face honest. Always position a mirror adjacent to your office telephone. Never take or make a call without checking out your mirror. Cicero once said, "Your face is your own fault after forty." In sales, your face and smile are your responsibilities on every sales call.

What you're looking for when you sneak a peek at your mirror is your facial expression, especially your smile. A small smile can warm up a big room and a cold customer. Do your best before every sales call to sneak a peek at your reflection. Attitude adjustments work best before the call is made, not after. Another way to measure your smile factor is to look at your customer. If he's smiling, you probably are; and if he's not you definitely aren't. When a customer wants to get down to business and talk price, you can expect his smile to disappear. A lower price concession from you, might bring it back, and so will your smile. Use your smile as a negotiating tool to warm up the meeting, and you might even get a better price for your product.

Smiling is to winning what frowning is to losing. Sorry, there are no choices here; if you want to win more sales, smile more often. It pays better too.

In 1975 I learned a valuable lesson from one of my customers. His name was John. At the time, I was a sales rep for the Scientific Products Division of American Hospital Corporation. The division I worked for distributed laboratory supplies, chemicals, and equipment and sold these products to industrial research and quality control laboratories.

One of my newly assigned accounts was General Foods, located in Tarrytown, New York, just east of the Tappan Zee bridge near the Hudson River. It was a beautiful campus with a speed limit of 19 mph. For some reason I remember the speed limit, I believe it has to do with the power of odd numbers. John had spent his entire career as a laboratory tech. The current buyer at the time of my first sales call was Brian.

I'll never forget my first sales call on Brian. I can't forget it, because it was the only time he came out to see me. During that first call, Brian came out to see me in the main reception area. Remember, I was real new in that position, and Brian did everything he could to make me feel uncomfortable. He told me the only reason he'd ever buy anything from my company, was if he desperately needed it and no one else had it in stock. That was the end of the conversation. No explanations were offered, though I tried to find out what created the problem. With all due respect to the theory that persistence pays off, sometimes it doesn't and sometimes you must adjust your thinking to patience pays off. Well, I did and it did.

Within a year, Brian retired. Sometimes that's what it takes to get your new foot into an old door. At the time General Foods had a "promote from within" policy. They posted the buyer's job. Several people applied and John was selected. His mandate, from Brad the purchasing agent, was to shake things up. I guess Brad had suspected that things were too cozy, a little stagnant and ready for some changes.

Once John got situated in his position, he called in some new suppliers. I was one of them, and unlike my experience with Brian, John and I connected immediately. We both had, "Gee, I'm new - maybe we can help each other" attitudes. John began to give me purchase orders. Initially, they weren't big, but they were orders. They were also problem items. I worked my hardest to solve his problem orders. The more problems I solved, the more orders I received that weren't problems.

John was unique in several ways. I remember that his passion was sailing. He had a thirty-five foot sailboat moored on the Hudson River. Another passion of John's was eating. It was this passion that helped teach me an invaluable lesson that I want to share with you. Even though John was new in his position, he took advantage of every opportunity to go out to lunch with salespeople. During all those years working in the labs, and hearing how often the buyers went out to lunch with salespeople, he was determined to get his share of the lunches, now that he was a buyer. It was during one of these lunches, that I learned a lesson on attitude.

As we waited for our meals to be served, John commented on how he really enjoyed having lunch with me. I immediately returned the compliment and told him that I enjoyed his company too. He said he really meant it and it wasn't a

33

patronizing comment. He proceeded to describe a lunch he had with my competitor the previous week. During that lunch, the salesman told John the intimate details of the divorce he was going through. He talked about the custody battle he and his wife were going through over their fifteen month old son. He further explained how hurt, tormented and torn-up he was over the whole thing. According to John, the salesman went on to describe how it was affecting his appetite, sleep at night and even his job performance. John said, "I was practically in tears listening to the gory details."

Well, after John shared that experience with me, he looked at me with a smile and said, "Going out to lunch with you is different. We get away from the office, have a few laughs and get to know each other a little better. This is what a business lunch is supposed to be like."

Do you think my competitor ever discovered the impact that lunch had on John? Of course not. Do you think he ever imagined that particular lunch was such a downer for John? Of course not. He confused sharing personal problems with building rapport and establishing a good working relationship with a new customer. Attitude is really everything. Make sure yours is adjusted before every sales call. Always remember it's "show time" before you make a sales call.

That's the story and here's the take away for you. Whenever you're in a situation having to deal with personal problems at home, no matter what they are, you have two choices and only two choices when you're making sales calls. You can either affect or infect your customers. Your attitude makes the difference. Your customers have their own problems, don't add yours to theirs. Be as positive as you can be, in a genuine way, and your customers will always look forward to your next visit.

John and I shared many lunches and did lots of business together.

Part II

Get A Grip On Your Life
Don't Quadruple Your Efforts

9. Plan: Use a map

If you want to double your sales, create a plan to do it. Success shouldn't depend on luck. Oh, you can get lucky, I'm just suggesting there's a better way. The better way relies on a map. In the future, consider your MAP as My Action Plan. Maps are handy guideposts. You'll get to your destination more quickly when you use a map. Maps plot the path and show the way. Don't limit your use of maps to planning vacations. Your MAP will become your compass to success. Remember, all maps are in writing. They don't have to be long and complicated. All you need to start using maps is a starting point and a destination. Consider using maps for your: life, business, family, physical well-being, personal finances, brainpower, and everyday activities.

For Your Life
Regardless of your age, prepare a list of all the things you want to do while you're still a consumer of oxygen. Review it periodically and concentrate on the most important items. It's your life, why shouldn't you spend it working your list and personalized MAP.

For Your Business
Prepare a list of all your business goals. Add these items (objectives) to your list: income, sales, profit, margin, market share, product mix, new accounts opened, regional performance ranking, divisional performance ranking, and company-wide performance ranking. Consider where you are in these critical areas, then plan for where you want to be. Your MAP creates the path and minimizes the obstacles.

For Your Family
Why have a MAP for your business and not for your family? Never put your family on the back burner. Your family doesn't want your success, they need your time. Your family deserves a prominent position on all your MAPs.

For Your Physical Well-Being
The quickest way to the cemetery is to neglect physical conditioning. As humans, we have input and output. Here's an idea. Get naked, and stand before a full length mirror. If you like what you see, go to the next paragraph. If you don't, get a MAP for getting back into shape. You'll feel better, look better, and perform better in the competitive arena on a daily basis.

For Your Personal Finances
If you know your net worth, do you have a specific net worth goal? There are three principle ways to acquire significant wealth. First, you can inherit it. Since people are living longer, and if you are in line to inherit, you may have to wait longer. Second, you can win the lottery. Third, and this is a no-brainer, you can plan to save for it. With savings and compounding you can become wealthy over time. The more time you give it, the more wealth you'll accumulate. Your

financial MAP should be a net worth spreadsheet that's updated monthly and reevaluated annually.

For Increasing Your Brainpower
Don't limit the acquisition of knowledge to personal experience. Most salespeople are busy. Most salespeople also have more than enough windshield time. Convert your car into a classroom. Listen to audio cassette tapes for fifteen minutes every day. Read fifteen pages of business related material or read for fifteen minutes every day. The MAP to doubling your sales depends on constant and continuous learning. With a mind full of new ideas, you can easily make continuous and gradual improvements.

For Your Everyday Activities
Perhaps the most important MAP you use is your written daily plan. Proactive salespeople schedule their priorities and take control of their schedule. Each day map out what you want to do, who you need to see, and who you must call. Don't let the daily distractions take you off the course you set for the day. Your MAP will keep you on track. Here's the choice. Do you want your MAP or the distractions to rule the day? Today, there are too many distractions and not enough MAPs.

Throughout this book you'll get more ideas about your MAPs. A day without a MAP is an opportunity to get lost. It's always more fun to know where you're going. Getting there is half the fun. The journey always precedes the destination. Plan yours carefully.

10. Time: Make every tick count

Time is of the essence, isn't it? What's important in your professional and personal life? Time is critical and essential to selling success. Unfortunately, time is a limited resource. Don't expect any more than the twenty-four hours each of us is given at the start of every day. This precious time is your daily allotment. You have unlimited choices each day. You can use time or you can waste time. You can prioritize what you will do with your time, or you can let time dribble by and squander it forever.

"Time management" is at best a myth and at worst an oxymoron. You have zero control over the speed of time. You can't speed it up or slow it down. You are relegated to winding up the old grandfather's clock and changing the batteries in your watch. Your control over time is nonexistent. How you use your time is an exercise in self-control. Sadly, most folks don't score well in this category, because it requires discipline and diligence.

Do you know the answers to these questions without having to do the math?

> Fifteen minutes is what percent of a twenty-four hour day?

> Fifteen minutes is what percent of an eight hour day?

How many minutes are there in a day?

How many hours are there in a week?

What's the average life expectancy for a male/female?

How much time do you have left?

Most folks don't have a clue to the answers because they macro-manage their time. The macro's waste a lot of time. The micro's compartmentalize everything they do and they typically get more done. The difference between the two is small yet staggering. It's small because minor changes are easy to adopt. It's staggering because these adaptations to your schedule can dramatically change your life forever.

Here's a timely dozen. Twelve ideas, easy to incorporate, that can dramatically impact your selling results, your family and your fun.

1. Set your alarm clock for thirty minutes earlier each day of the week. Do the math and see how much extra time it gives you. How you use the extra time is up to you.

2. Begin every day with a written "To Do" list. Your list should contain all the things you want to do, all the people you want to call, all the phone numbers for all the people you want to call, and the six most important items on your list must be prioritized.

3. Think of your calendar as the center of your life. Identify what's important to you and always put those things on your calendar. Your family belongs on your calendar. Your vacations, exercise, reading, and hobbies belong there too. If your calendar controls your days, make sure you're headed in the right direction.

4. Build time cushions into your calendar every day. A little elasticity goes a long way in a hectic lifestyle.

5. Read every day. Not reports, but personal growth material. If you don't nurture yourself, you won't grow. Take notes when reading to capture good ideas.

6. Don't let a day go by without asking "Is there a better way?" If there is a better way, make the changes. Don't wait for someone to hand you a "passport" to enter the world of change.

7. Wear a watch and watch your watch. It's mindless to wear a watch and not pay attention to it. Being on time says a lot about your consistency and credibility. Being late says something too.

8. Delegate more. Forget Lone Ranger selling. Don't do anything if someone else can do it for you. You can't double your sales if you're doing a lot of non-selling stuff. Your highest priority is to be face-to-face with your customers.

9. When you go on vacations don't call the office. They'll survive without you. You'll also send your family a powerful message about their importance.

10. Take good notes. If it's noteworthy, write it down.

11. Buy new technology only when it simplifies your life. You can do without it if it's going to complicate things.

12. Clean your office, your brief case and your car quarterly. Toss out everything that's not essential to your personal and professional life. Clutter is a distraction. It's not about you knowing where something is. Clutter sends the wrong message to everyone who sees it.

Remember, fifteen minutes is 1% of a twenty-four hour day.

Remember, fifteen minutes is 3% of an eight hour work day.

Remember, there are 1440 minutes in a day.

Remember, there are 168 hours in a week.

Subtract your age from your life expectancy and multiply by twelve to determine your life expectancy in months. Men use seventy-six years and women use seventy-nine years. Don't put off living. Life isn't a dress rehearsal and no one gets out alive. If you pack every day with the right stuff, you'll live a longer and better life.

11. Reactivity: Quit chasing your tail

Which would you rather be, proactive or reactive? I can imagine your response. Next question, which are you, proactive or reactive? Maybe it depends on how you spend your days. Use a quarter to draw a circle in the center of the page on a sheet of paper. Using your pen or pencil, shade in the entire circle. Above the circle write the word "button." To the left of the word button, write the word "reactive" and to the right of the word button write "proactive."

Who pushes the button determines whether you're proactive or reactive. If you push the button and begin working on a specific high priority task, you are proactive. On the other hand, if someone else pushes the button and you begin working immediately on his request, without regard and consideration of your priorities, you are reactive.

Under the word "reactive," prepare a list of things that make you reactive. For example, the telephone rings and someone beckons with a request. Your pager starts to vibrate indicating a number for you to call immediately. You check e-mails only to find half of them asking you to do something. A demanding customer makes an unreasonable request. Your manager loads one task upon another on you. This is not a pretty picture. If your typical day looks like this, don't even begin to think you're a proactive person. You're being extremely reactive, if you spend your days responding to the button that other people are pushing.

Under the word "proactive," prepare a list of things to turn these reactive situations into proactive opportunities. When someone calls with a request, politely and firmly let him know what you're working on and when you'll be able to deal with his request. He may not like it, but most folks settle for second best when their first request isn't possible or even practical. Giving people your pager number is tantamount to telling them that they can have instant access to you which means they can expect to hear from you within an hour. One proud and naive sales rep told me he gave his pager number to 250 customers. Just imagine what his days are like. If you must use a pager, give the number to your spouse, three large customers and three large prospects. When the pager goes off, you'll know it's important.

E-mails should be checked twice a day. You should be able to tell by the return addresses, if it's something to open and respond to immediately. If in doubt, let it wait. There's a huge difference between really good customer service and dropping everything to respond to every customer request. Like everything else, customer requests should be prioritized. Tell a customer the earliest you'll be able to respond to his request or if possible redirect him to someone else in your company. Don't be the Lone Ranger when dealing with customer requests. Platoon Selling over the long haul is more advantageous to you and your customers. Learn to delegate more. Don't ever do something that you can ask someone else in your company to do, simply because you can do it better and quicker. Proactive people schedule their priorities and then work them.

Dogs aren't the only ones to chase their tails. Reactive people chase around in circles every day instead of focusing their efforts on items of the highest priority. Then they rationalize the energy they've expended by reflecting on how busy they have been. The built-in beauty with priorities, is that you get to select what's important and when you want to work on them.

Nothing produces better results than beginning each day with a six-pack. This six-pack is a list of six important tasks that you've prioritized for the day. When something happens during the day and hits the fan, don't touch it unless it's more important than your six-pack of priorities. Start your day with a six-pack and you'll spend less time chasing your tail.

> *Time is the scarcest resource and unless it is managed, nothing else can be managed.*
> *Peter Drucker*

> *Spilled water never returns to the cup.*
> *Japanese Proverb*

12. Communication: Get stylish

To achieve selling success, real achievers must first know themselves and how they communicate. Real achievers must also know their customers and how they communicate. Finally to achieve consistent and credible success, real achievers must be able to adapt their style to their customers' styles.

There are many ways to assess your behavior selling style which is based on your communication style. One of the best ways is to take a personal inventory using the Personal Insights Profile, a DISC* instrument. For a small investment you can harvest big dividends. DISC is about the universal language of behavior and emotions. It is the language of "how we act." DISC profiles people as directors, interactors, servers or compliers based on human behaviors.

There are several benefits to finding out which one you are. Chief among the benefits is gaining insights about your selling style. The more you know about yourself, the more likely it is that your income will increase, that your sales will increase, and that your customers will be more satisfied with their working relationship with you.

Research has validated that people tend to buy from salespeople with behavioral styles similar to their own. When salespeople can adapt their behavior styles to that of the customers, sales increase.

All selling is based on five premises of human behavior:

1. You cannot motivate another person, you can only create an environment in which people become self motivated.
2. All people are capable of being motivated and will do things for reasons which appeal to them - not you.
3. A person's strengths overextended, may become a weakness.
4. If a person understands himself better than you understand yourself, then that person will control the situation.
5. If a person understands himself and understands you better than you understand yourself, then that person can control you.

DISC can't measure intelligence, personality, values, education, training, skills, or experience. It does, however, measure observable behavior and emotions. See if knowing a little bit about DISC can work for you.

The "D" personality has a need to direct and dominate others. His dominant strength is his ego and task orientation. He loves to be personally challenged.

The "I" likes to interact with other people. His major strength is his optimism and people orientation. He needs to be recognized for his effort and achievement.

The "S" has a need to serve others. His dominant strength is that he's a team player and very results-oriented. He is driven by traditional practices.

The "C" is a complier. His dominant strength is accuracy and intuitiveness. He's driven to do things the correct and precise way; he has very high standards.

Real achievers always know themselves. Real achievers realize and understand that knowing themselves is not enough to achieve selling success. Real achievers attempt to get to know their customers. A professional sales representative will want to know the buying habits of each behavior style. Here are some examples. The "D" likes new and unique products and looks for results. They like to make quick decisions. The "I" likes showy and flashy products and is looking for the experience to be fun. They also make quick decisions. The "S" likes traditional products. They're looking for trust in salespeople and they make decisions slowly. The "C" likes products that are proven and time-tested. They always want more information and make decisions slowly.

How good are you at reading people. Here are some clues to watch for as you interact with your customers and potential customers. The "D" is likely to be extroverted, task-oriented, very direct, impatient, results-focused, always in a hurry, efficient, not neat, a high risk taker, a rule breaker, likes to get to the point, avoids chit chat, and is always going somewhere. Here's how to recognize the "I." He's likely to be extroverted, people-oriented, slightly disorganized, likes to have fun in relationships, is very visual, a moderate risk-taker, is not always aware of the rules, likes long conversations.

The "S" is introverted, people-oriented, indirect, trusting, does not like change, enjoys a relaxed pace, usually relies on some type of system, is a low risk-taker, follows time-tested rules, and is a warm conversationalist.

The "C" tends to be introverted, very task-oriented, indirect in his communication style, likes procedures, requires lots of information, is highly organized, does not like risk-taking, likes to get to the point, and do things "by the book."

Real achievers, who know themselves and their customers, recognize there's more work to be done. It's not enough to know your customer, it's equally as important to adapt your selling style to the customer's style - especially if your style doesn't match his. Here are some ideas on adapting your style.

Adapting to a "D" usually means you're dealing with a person with a big ego. They do not like to waste time. They don't want lots of facts and figures. They are more impressed with a very efficient and businesslike approach. A good way to motivate them is to say something like, "You'll want to try this out." When speaking to the "D" make sure your choices are very direct and always emphasize results and bottom-line. Avoid being indecisive. Answer objections directly. Don't get into long, detailed scenarios or presentations. Typical questions you can expect to be asked by a "D" include: "What does it cost?" "Is this the best model?" "Can I change it?"

Adapting to the "I" means you'll be dealing with a friendly person who is glad to see you and will want to trade jokes. "I's" are likely to buy quickly, so spare the details. Allow time for socializing; offer to take the person to lunch. A statement that could be very motivating for an "I" is typically something like, "This product allows you and your company to lead the way into the future." Be sure that you're enthusiastic and having fun. Give the "I" lots of choices. Don't let him talk too much or you could find yourself off-track and losing the sale. Use the "I's" own words and questions to keep him on track.

When you're trying to adapt to an "S," recognize that he will have a high need to trust the salesperson calling on him. The "S" may also be very shy. Take it slow and easy. Provide plenty of proof and statistics. A statement that's potentially motivating to a "S" is, "Call some of our customers who are currently using our products to determine their satisfaction." Throughout the selling process, be sincere by using a quiet manner and do not try the hard-sell approach. Be sure to give assurances that his decision is the right one and always provide full explanations.

Adapting to the "C" personality means you can expect your potential customer to be suspicious of you and your products. "C's" do not easily make changes to new suppliers, and they will require lots of proof and background information. They will also need lots of time to absorb the details and facts before going to the next step. A statement that might motivate a "C" is, "Once you've taken the time to examine the facts, you'll see this is right for you." Throughout your presentation be sure to present your ideas in a non-threatening way. Seek to find ways to minimize your potential customer's risk. Avoid getting too personal too quickly. Also avoid loud or emotional sales presentations, they simply do not work with a "C."

Winning more sales requires extra effort. To know yourself, make sure you take a personal inventory of your selling style. To know your customer and his buying style, be sure you sharpen your observation and listening skills. Once you are aware of your selling style and have successfully identified your customer's buying style, all that remains is for you to adapt your style to his style. A knowledge of communication styles will lead to more sales and a bigger income.

DISC - Copyright 1994, Target Training International, Ltd.

13. Controllables:
Start managing what you can

If you are a salesperson and you're driving down the rocky road of life, ask yourself, "Are you in control?" Judging from the results of my national survey, a majority of you would say "no." In business, especially in sales, there is nothing worse than the low, sinking, "walls moving in" kind of feeling when there is more piled on your "To Do" list than the available time needed even to put a dent in it?

If you consider the profession of sales and all its complexity, you can simplify your approach by dividing sales into four major components. The most important component is you and how you manage yourself, your time and your activities. The second component is filled with your accounts and everything about them from basic account information to strategic sales plans. The third component consists of the turf and geography you cover. Geographic coverage relates specifically to how well you schedule your calls and how much time you spend behind the wheel or in front of potential customers. The last component consists of your personal selling process. The secret to success is to balance preparation with improvisation. Let's review each component in more detail.

Self-management
Have you ever thought about things like "getting a grip, getting a life, and having more quiet time?" If you have these thoughts often, you might be out-of-control. Don't worry,

you're not alone. But what can you do about it? For starters, consider using a watch, an electronic organizer and a daily, weekly, and monthly written plan.

You might be wearing a watch and not using it. A professional is early or on time. If you don't periodically look at your watch to keep you on track and on time, you'll end up being late and rushing. Your watch may be a piece of fine jewelry, but it should function as a time piece. Divide your day into bite size manageable pieces. Remember fifteen minutes is three percent of an eight-hour day.

Post-it notes are colorful little pieces of paper that are great for reminders and terrible for managing your time and your life. Get an electronic organizer. Any software program that allows you to plan daily, weekly, monthly, and annual events will suffice. Rewriting a daily "To Do" list is unnecessary today. Any task not complete automatically gets added to tomorrow's list. Using a software program to organize your schedule, will automate your record keeping, help with correspondence, and put all customer information at your finger tips.

You must have a written plan. First you need a written plan for your life. Your life, personally and professionally will be chaotic and more stressful without a game plan. Why write down a plan for minor events such as a visit to the grocery store or a list of activities to do on a vacation, and not have a written plan for your life. If you live life one day at a time, I think that's how we do it, it's critical to plan each day carefully. Don't limit your daily plan to a long list of activities, include quiet time, creative time, exercise time and also family time. You'll feel more in control.

Account management

There are large accounts and small accounts. The large ones buy more, so I'll emphasize them. The concept is equally well-suited for small accounts, but it doesn't pay as much. Think of each of your accounts as a silo. Each silo is filled with opportunities for you. The best way to manage your silos is to begin with a blueprint.

This silo blueprint reveals structure and landscape. Every silo has an organization. A key to successfully working with an account is to discover how it is organized. Start with the company's mission and vision statements. Try to get an organization chart to see the vertical and horizontal layout. Uncover the company's financials to assess underlying strengths and weaknesses. Examine the company's share in the market it serves, and determine their biggest customers and competitors.

Every organization has people. Obtain complete contact information for as many different people that buy, use, influence and make decisions for your product. Get to the decision makers first and get to them early. Decision makers have the power and usually delegate the work. Sometimes they're more accessible than their staffs, who are busy being worker bees. Always aim high early in the selling cycle.

In your portfolio of account information include key people. Profile the decision makers. Make note of their communication style (dominant, expressive, amiable or analytical) so you can adapt your style to their style.

In large accounts it's easy to focus on a few key people and lose contact with others. Develop a plan for staying connected with everyone in the account. E-mail and voice mail are great tools for staying connected and so are newsletters. If your company doesn't have one yet, don't wait, create your own. Desktop publishing software packages like Quark and Page Maker, with their built-in templates, make this a snap to do and cost effective as well.

When you're working large accounts, always focus on the relationship curve. Where are you in building key relationships? Relationships are built on effective communication, added value, and building trust with the people in the silo. Sometimes you can jump-start the relationship building process by getting your key contacts out of their silo. Breakfasts, lunches, dinners, and visits to your company facilities often go a long way in the relationship department and so does a round of golf.

Don't make the mistake of spending too much time with too few people. It's strategic suicide to invest too much time with the people who aren't the true decision makers. Start with a blueprint and you'll build better relationships.

Territory Management

There are two critical components to effective territory management and they're as close as kissing cousins. The first is face-to-face time in front of your prospects and customers. The second is routing and scheduling the way you do it. If you're not good at the second, you'll never maximize the first.

Do you know how many days a year you are in front of your prospects and customers? Most salespeople don't keep score and that's a costly mistake. Ignorance is never bliss when it comes to wasting time.

Take a guess. Write down the number of days a year you believe you are in front of your prospects and customers. Use the space provided.

_____

This number represents your perception. What's more important is your reality number. In the space provided enter the number of days.

How many weekend days are there in a year?   _____

How many vacation days do you get each year?   _____

How many paid personal and holidays
are you entitled to?   _____

How many home office / administrative days
do you take a year?   _____

How many days do you spend attending
meetings and training programs?   _____

How many sick days do you take each year?   _____

How many lost days (weather, canceled appointments,
Christmas week) do you take?   _____

Total: _____

Add up all these days and subtract from 365. You are left with your reality number. This reality number represents the number of days available to make your numbers. If you multiply your reality number by your average number of daily sales calls, you can calculate your annual sales call numbers.

Once you have calculated total days and total sales calls, you can divide your sales quota dollars by each number. A street smart salesperson knows the value of each day and every sales call, shouldn't you? If you have a variable income, it varies based on performance. Divide your target annual income for this year by the number of days you have available. You should know how much you earn each day. You can also divide your income goal by the annual number of sales calls you expect to make to derive income per sales call numbers.

If you keep records for your automobile mileage, divide monthly business miles driven by the total number of sales calls made. This will provide a miles per account barometer, which when checked monthly can indicate ups and downs to avoid developing bad habits.

In addition to knowing your numbers there are seven practical steps to managing your territory more effectively.

1. Prioritize all accounts, customers and prospects (Large, Medium and Small).

2. Establish a call frequency schedule for each classification of account - large, medium and small.

3. Determine in advance the percentage of your time you'll commit to prospecting.

4. Change your call pattern to maximize face-to-face selling time.

5. Remember 80% of your revenue comes from 20% of your customers.

6. Remember, 80% of your prospect's potential comes from 20% of your prospects.

7. Never leave home without a map, written call objectives, and a written territory plan.

Territory management is an essential step to achieving sales success in your territory. It starts with knowledge. Do the math to determine where you are currently. Do your very best to convert driving time to selling time and family time. Everything around you is changing. It's okay to change your call schedule, if it makes you more productive. The customer you always see on Mondays may be a better customer if you called on him on Thursday afternoons. You wouldn't let anyone steal your wallet. Don't let anyone steal your time.

Time is money. It always has been and it always will be.

Sales call management
What is your response to this questions, "What's your recipe for selling?" Do you have a response? Do you abide by a formal sales process? Does it consist of multiple steps that are thoughtfully mapped out in writing? Does this sales process suit you and fit your products? What percentage of your sales calls are prepared versus improvised?

I'd like to share my sales process with you. It's easy to use and hard to do without. It has seven steps, each one different from the other yet very much connected.

1. The selling process always begins with networking. To build your network, you must cast the net. All fishermen understand that fish don't jump onto boats voluntarily.

2. The selling process always asks the right questions. A sales person without questions is like a comedian without jokes. Questions if used properly get you off the hook. No salesperson worth his salt wants to talk about products before he knows what the customer needs. Asking questions, open-ended ones, gets the job done.

3. The selling process always depends on effective listening. Listening is activated in two ways. First, it kicks in whenever you ask a really good question. Second, once you've asked your question, listening is also activated by closing your mouth. When the mouth is in the closed position, the ears work wonderfully. Another way to boost your listening skills is to take notes.

4. The selling process always uncovers specific problems and opportunities. Unlike most doctors, salespeople seem to prefer talking about their prescriptions before they do the examination. Be like a doctor. Do the exam before you offer your product as the cure.

5. The selling process always presents tailored solutions. One size never fits all, so present only tailor-made solutions to your customers. This involves doing more homework initially. Don't leave a customer trying to imagine if your product will work. Show him specifically, in the context of his problems, how your product works to his advantage. A sale occurs when your product solves the customer's specific problem. It's the relatability factor. Before the customer can relate to your product, you must relate to his problem or special situation.

6. The selling process always deals with concerns. There are four universal objections. No money, no need, no hurry, and no confidence. Conceptually, learn how to deal with each. The best objections to get are the ones you get often. Recurring objections are gifts, because you know you'll get them over and over. You can't prepare for the objection you haven't heard before. You can prepare and practice for the one you'll hear again tomorrow. How could you intelligently not want to prepare for an objection you know you'll hear again, probably next week.

7. The selling process always secures the commitment. Asking for the business doesn't take guts, it takes know-how. When it's time to ask for the business, how specifically do you ask? If you have to think about it, it means you don't know. There are no techniques for asking for the business, only words. Think about the words you'll use. Write them down on a sheet of paper. Play with

the words. Only keep the words that are essential. Recite them out loud. Listen to how they sound. You'll know when you have the best combination of words. It'll sound like music. Before you get to the account, rehearse these words a minimum of six times. Keep doing it until you can do it without inserting any "um's" and "ah's". Imagine how good you'll feel and sound, when you're in front of the customer. You'll be extremely confident, because you've already practiced it six times. Going for the order shouldn't create anxiety, it should get you the business.

The selling process is just that - a process. It's not a mish mash, an improvisation or a comedy act. It always starts with your customer and ideally ends with your product positioned as a tailor-made solution. The secret to success is to balance preparation with spontaneity, to do the homework before taking the exam and to realize that selling is more about skills than instinct.

14. Goals: Use them to make a difference

If there is one thing that symbolizes the Olympics for me, it has to be the Torch. In 1996 at the Summer Olympics, Americans had the opportunity to carry the torch across our country to the site of the Atlanta games. The Torch is a metaphor for our lives. When we are born, our Torch is lit. When we die, the flame flickers and finally peters out.

During our lives we carry a big, bright, burning Torch. If you know where you're going, it lights the way. If, on the other hand, your destination is unclear, all pathways you take have light but no direction. In seminar after seminar I present, countless salespeople sit starry-eyed while I discuss the importance and significance of preparing goals. When a power point is made or an example is given, they nod in unison and convince themselves that they will make goal-setting a part of their planning ritual.

The choice is really quite simple. You're either dream-oriented or goal-focused. It doesn't take a lot to be dream oriented. Fill your mind with idle fantasy and your days with random spontaneity. Plan little and accept what comes along- that's a dreamer for you.

Most goals have their beginnings as dreams, but there is a conversion process. Five simple steps that can achieve the unbelievable, overcome the impossible, and for some, change lives forever.

The five steps to perfect goal-setting are:

1. Goals are goals, only if they're in writing.

2. Goals must be specific and measurable. If you can't measure it, you might not achieve it.

3. Goals must have completion dates, in writing. The date should include the day, month and year.

4. Goals should make you stretch. Don't make them too easy to achieve.

5. Picturize all goals. If you can't see them, you can't be guided by them.

Five easy steps. Easy to say and easy to do. What's stopping you? Procrastinators are always thinking about tomorrow. Results-oriented salespeople are doing it today.

We are each given the opportunity to chart our destiny. Why leave everything to chance? Consider your future carefully and plan it wisely. Make today the best day of your week.

Remember your Torch. Aim it toward your goals; let it brighten your path, while the light is still yours.

15. Focus: Write yourself a check

There are three principal "givens" in sales. The first is you are "given" a quota. You almost always think it's too high and slightly unfair. The second "given" is, you usually are "given" your quota late. Few sales managers and companies they work for are ahead of this curve. For example, if you're on a calendar fiscal year, you're likely to get your quota late January, February, or even as late as March. Makes sense that you are given ten or eleven months to achieve your new annual quota. The third "given" is that most salespeople will naturally focus on achieving the quota they are "given."

Your quota is the desired outcome. That's what you aim for. In a different chapter I discussed the reason why you should adjust your aim. If you achieve your quota it impacts your income. There is a direct relationship between outcomes and incomes. It could be argued that outcomes influence incomes and indeed they do. The larger the outcome the bigger the income.

Here's a thought to consider. Incomes are also a powerful motivator, especially if you use post-dated checks. Why wait until the end of the year to see how much you'll make. For most salespeople, income opportunities are quite variable and quite dependent on your performance (outcomes). If you want to earn more you must sell more. Start with your income, not with your outcome. Here's what to do.

Make a photo copy of a blank check from your check register. Once copied, cut out the copy of the check so it's actually sized like your checks are. Here's a checklist of what you need to do.

1. Write your name in the appropriate space.

2. Enter the date for the last day of your current fiscal year. For most of you, it will be December 31st.

3. Enter the dollar amount in the spaces provided. Include the alpha and numeric amounts.

4. Sign the check.

5. Have three copies of the check laminated. One for your office, one for your car, and one for your briefcase.

6. Look at it daily.

7. When you cash it, spend it wisely.

Don't be paralyzed by the quota you're given. Immediately convert it to your income objective, and get your creative juices flowing. You'll be more creative if you concentrate on your personal income goal than if you focus merely on the quota you are given.

If you want to be inspired, get wired. Make sure your income is wired to your quota. If you focus on how to earn your income goal, you'll be better positioned to achieve your quota. Focus on your income like a laser beam and you'll always achieve your quota.

16. Technology: Keep it in check

Oh, what a beautiful day it is. To be able to do so much with so many technological choices, I haven't been this euphoric since I was sixteen and got my driver's license. According to Clint Willis, a writer for *Forbes Magazine*, "Embedded chips will heal your body, drive your car, and transform your work. They'll also find you a parking spot and make you a better skier."

In a recent article, Willis listed twenty-five things that are on the horizon and likely to change our lives including: toxin testers, automotive auto pilot, bionic eyes, common cold detectors, smart clothes, intelligent houses, earthquake survivor detectors, wearable computers, all-knowing appliances, injectable health monitors and even smart skis.

On the surface it sounds remarkable if not wonderful. I get excited just thinking about all this new stuff. Before you run out and hoist a beer in celebration of the coming new wave of techno gizmos, consider this first. All this new technology will be added to the already busy schedule you have. It will be added to the twenty-five e-mails you're getting daily. It'll be added to the thirty voice mails you're getting. They will be added to the audio e-mails you're getting and will be added to the daily video conferences you're likely to be scheduling in the very near future.

The basic problem with technology is that there are too many choices. For example, salespeople can be more productive if they automate many of their activities. But where do you begin, and once you're up and running, how do you continue to make sensible choices to sustain continuous improvement in your business?

Starting with computer hardware, you can order scores of different systems. You can buy them or lease them. You can order a computer from a department store, a specialty computer store, a catalog or the company's web site. I bought my first MAC from a department store twelve years ago and purchased my new PC from Dell via the Internet. What kind of a system do you need? Generally, people buy desktops first. Once acclimated to the system, the hooks are in now, you begin think more about size and weight. The second purchase is the Notebook. The third purchase is the Palm-size computer. And the Dick Tracy watch is coming soon. The choices are limitless, especially when you consider that according to forecasters, five years from now, embedded chips costing $25 will be more powerful than today's best Pentiums.

Software presents even more choices for the professional sales representative. You'll have to consider software for word processing, spread sheets, account management, database management, desk-top publishing, presentations, territory management, voice activation, organization calendars, personal finances, and web-authoring. If that isn't mind boggling, you're routinely enticed and encouraged to upgrade your software to remove old problems and add the newest, latest, greatest features you can't possible do without.

I could never go back to the days of pencil and paper. Technology and all that it inspires has many benefits. It also can create absolute havoc if you're not patient and careful. Being patient means integrating technology gradually, continuously, and if possible seamlessly with the way you currently do business. You must be careful not to take the technology learning curve out of family time. Technology is like a black hole in space, it's limitless. So what's the rush?

As you race around, trying to put new techno toys in your shopping basket, consider these three points.

1. Does the new techno toy simplify or complicate your life? Life means both personal and professional. Does it add value, save time, save money, and otherwise make you a better person? If it doesn't, you don't need it.

2. When you buy this techno toy, will you classify it as an investment or as an expense? Expenses get written off and investments are expected to generate returns to the investor. What's the R.O.I. going to be on your family life, your territory and overall professional performance. Make certain the anticipated return justifies your initial investment. If it doesn't, you don't need it.

3. Will the purchase of this techno toy increase or decrease the balance you currently have in your life? Since most of us are already struggling to maintain a reasonable balance between our professional and personal lives, make sure your purchase is able to increase and not going to decrease the balance you have in your life. If it doesn't, you don't need it.

Time is an essential resource. On the surface, technology can provide a big boost to your personal and professional productivity. Remember, computers were designed and promoted to reduce the need for paper. Technology must be properly harnessed, or like anything else it has the potential to go wild on you.

Sitting down is the ideal position to be using your computer. Standing up and getting to see more customers should be a higher priority. Don't let sitting in front of your computer interfere with family time and watching the kids grow up time. Your real net value to your family is measured in terms of the time you spend with them not with the things you buy for them.

17. Names: Fatten your Rolodex

Names and faces are what's important. Early on in my sales career, I was told to get the names, then arrange to see the faces, and then make sure in the future I could connect the names with the faces. That was old fashioned networking.

I'd like to say it hasn't changed much, but it has. Networking is more important today than ever before. In the past, one network was sufficient, today you need a minimum of three. The networks should be built around your customers, your company, and your personal resource connections.

Customer networks should be built vertically and horizontally. Once you have this V/H mentality, it doesn't matter who the first name is or what he does, he will be the source for additional names within that organization. Focus on adding vertical and horizontal names. Last week during a seminar, I asked a participant how many people he personally knew in the steel mill he was calling on? How many people could he put a name to a face and be able to introduce me to them if we made a joint sales call. His response was "fifty." Now that's a prime example of a well-built customer network.

Yesterday's Rolodex card which had room for names, address and telephone numbers and little else won't cut it today. Fanning through your old card file to locate a name has gone the way of home delivery of milk and bread. Today's electronic Rolodex has room for so much more. In addition to name, address, telephone number, you'll want to add the FAX number, voice mail number, pager number, car phone, E-mail address, web site address, plus all the numbers your customer may be using from a home based office. Today's Rolodex also gives you ample space for personal information and anything at all you want to add to this profile.

Your company Rolodex should be built carefully and extensively. Remember networks work. They make things happen. Don't snuggle up with a handful of people and think you'll ever become a star. Stars get to be stars in part because they are master networkers. The best way to build a resource network within your company is to be a resource for others first. Go out of your way to meet people you don't know. Ask them about their responsibilities and challenges. Send them a handwritten note after your first meeting. Take a personal interest in everyone you meet; record key information on your Rolodex and you'll create a network beyond your imagination. Networks are great, but they have no initiative, that's your department. If there are 2,500 employees in your company and you know only forty-five people, you have a shabby network.

The third network is your personal resource network. It's everybody that you rely on personally and professionally to achieve your goals. It includes but is not limited to doctors, dentist, barber, beautician, mechanic, computer geek, computer repair person, plumber, electrician, politicians, butcher, and handyman. You should also include places like the bakery, clothing store, dry cleaners, newspaper office, auto dealership, and golf course. If you have to look these names and numbers up in a yellow page directory, you don't have a network.

To be really effective your networks should be wired and linked together. Networks need to grow and they need to be worked. Link your Network to your calendar. Remember birthdays, special events and holidays. As you meet new customers, new people in your company and identify new resource people, remember that the introduction is the beginning of the network relationship not the end. Master networkers work with and constantly interact with their networks.

The rapidity with which we forget is astonishing.
Dale Carnegie

A good beginning makes a good ending.
English Proberb

To be a success in business, be daring, be first, be different.
Henry Marchant

18. Score: Start keeping it

If you want to play ball, you'd better know the score. Like a professional athlete, you must know all your stats for the game you're playing.

In sales, there are primary areas on which to focus and collect statistics or measurements. First, you must focus on your customers and their specific needs. You're dead in the water if you don't. You must also focus on your products and services. If you know them inside out, you'll win more sales and do it more quickly. You must also focus on your performance. It's not enough, simply to know your performance to plan number.

If you become a master of measurement, you can dominate any market. The fact is, most salespeople don't pay attention to the details of their business. That sloppy approach to management and individual self-awareness creates an opportunity for you if you develop a spreadsheet mentality for your business.

I'm not an analytical type. You don't have to be, to recognize the power of numbers. The daily activities of a professional sales representative are easily quantified. If you're not looking (analyzing) at the right things, you may not be doing the right things either. Superiority never comes from mediocrity.

Jim Meisenheimer

Answer these questions to see if your examining the right stuff.

		Yes	No
1.	Do you have a spreadsheet for key selling activities?	____	____
2.	Do you know exactly how many names you have on your Rolodex?	____	____
3.	Do you know what percent of your time is allocated to customer and prospect sales calls?	____	____
4.	Do you know what your closing ratio percentage is?	____	____
5.	Do you know what your average selling cycle time is?	____	____
6.	Can you quickly recite your ten favorite open-ended questions without saying "um?"	____	____
7.	Do you know (to two decimal places) your overall gross profit margin?	____	____
8.	Do you know your specific (to two decimal places) product mix percentages for your emphasis products?	____	____

	Yes	No

9. Do you know your current percentage increase in sales versus prior year? _____ _____

10. Do you know your current sales dollar variance to prior year? _____ _____

11. Do you specifically know your margin variance numbers versus prior year? _____ _____

12. Do you know all the numbers for your top ten accounts? _____ _____

13. Do you know the answers to questions 7 - 10 for each of your ten largest accounts? _____ _____

14. Have you ever done the math to calculate how many days a year you spend in front of customers? (First subtract all vacation days, holidays, meeting days, home office days, sick days, lost days, etc.) _____ _____

15. Do you know how much your sales call productivity would increase for a year if you made one additional quality call per week? _____ _____

16. Do you know how many sales calls you made last year? _____ _____

	Yes	No
17. Do you know what your sales call productivity versus prior year is?	____	____
18. Do you record miles driven per month on a spreadsheet?	____	____
19. Do you know what your average dollars per sale numbers are?	____	____
20. Do you know your performance ranking compared to all other sales-people in your company?	____	____
Total	____	____

How many questions did you know the answer to? This isn't a game of twenty questions. If you were a professional golfer, baseball player, football player, or basketball player how many critical measurements would be scrutinized daily? The word "professional" adds a dimension of completeness and comprehensiveness that you don't expect to find with those people engaged in non-professional work.

Here are four guidelines for producing staggering sales results. It's work and time. Most of it comes in the set-up phase. Once you have it organized, it's easy to use.

First: Create a spreadsheet with at least twelve columns, one for each month. The rows should consist of the important measurements for you business.

Second: Update your numbers at least monthly and
             weekly if possible.

Third: Every month pinpoint your strengths and
             weaknesses.

Fourth: For every weakness prepare (in writing)
             three action steps to turn it around. Do
             your action steps without delay.

A sage once said, the best way out of a hole is to stop digging.
Efficient measurement is the first step to effective
management. Getting to the top requires a bottoms-up
approach. You can dominate your market, if you master the
measurables.

19: Investments: Reap the dividends

Do you have a computer? Do you have a car phone? In the last four years, I've asked those questions dozens of times. Many times, heads begin to nod and hands start to wave. Sometimes though, I get challenging comments, like "the company won't buy them for us," or "I'm waiting for the company to get them for us." These comments are especially mystifying when they come from straight commission salespeople who potentially have the most to gain from incremental performance enhancements.

How could a salesperson, who thinks so little of a company that denies him the benefits of state-of-the-art technology, not consider buying it himself if there so was so much to be gained? It's irrational, baffling and misdirected thinking.

Companies that invest in their employees are smart. Individuals that invest in themselves are even smarter. Today, as a sales representative, you're more than an employee; you're a free agent. The sky's the limit. Be ready for everything and anything. Your company successfully launches break-through products. Your company acquires other companies. Your company is acquired by an even larger company.

If you're just a mediocre sales rep you may not fit in. All the rules are changing. It's fair to say, particularly in business, there are no rules. Avoid clinging to the old ways of doing things. Forget thinking about what your company can do for you; actively consider what you can do for yourself.

There are four critical areas for you to consider making continuous investments in yourself. These investments are made with time and money, and in time they'll provide handsome dividends for you and your family.

Knowledge
The first and primary investment is in knowledge. Knowledge is the ultimate equalizer. Knowledge creates competitive advantage to those who employ it. There's a huge difference between data, information and knowledge. If you're like most salespeople, you're in-basket is overflowing with data and information. Once again, if you're like most salespeople, you probably didn't invest several thousand of your own dollars in the pursuit of knowledge.

Think of yourself as a brand or even as a company. How long could you survive, if you were always working with last year's knowledge? Not long, and you know it. If you spend a lot of time in your car, turn it into a classroom. Invest in one audio cassette tape each week. Listen to every tape you buy at least three times before you toss it into a shoe box. Subscribe to *Selling Power Magazine* (800-752-7355) and create an article file for these topics: negotiating, time management, attitude, motivation, writing proposals, networking, asking questions, presentation skills, handling concerns, and securing commitment. Read an article, then file it for future use. You literally become what you read and that's a scary thought if you don't read much. Invest in one seminar, workshop or course every year. Don't make food for your brain an optional entree. Feeding your brain is the quickest way to grow your business.

Technology

Invest in technology. Technology creates absolute power, when used properly. Technology is constantly changing. Be ready to invest a lot and be ready to invest often. Remember though, good investments provide great returns. Yesterday I got real excited when I down-loaded my audio e-mail file for the first time. I can now send anyone an audio e-mail. Video e-mail is next and on its heels you'll see video conferencing for all routine telephone calls. The main attraction, as I see it, for technology is speed. You can do everything faster and generally better. Technology magazines offer the best way to keep up on new trends and products. Every month buy two technology magazines. Scour them for what's new and exciting. Use the internet to stay on the leading edge of technology. There are two edges, leading and trailing. Each one has a distinct view. What do you want to be looking at tomorrow?

Balance

Invest in balance. All work and no play, means your stupid. At the very least it suggests you're not bright. After a seminar today, I had the opportunity to spend about twenty minutes talking with the company's top sales representative. His territory was in New York City. He said he was thirty-nine years old and he did very well in business but he had no personal life. He made a lot of money, more than any other sales rep in his company and he hadn't taken a vacation in three years. Hello! You can't save up relationships and vacations. You can't save up taking your spouse out to dinner. You can't save up watching your kids grow up. You can't save up going to Little League games. You can't save up playing golf and reading mystery novels. You can't save up taking Rover for long walks. You can't save up exercise. Get the point? Make some changes and seek out more ways to create balance in your life. Achieving balance today is a priority for a more healthy tomorrow. There are two edges to balance - personal and professional. Without proper balance, they both suffer and are diminished.

Yourself

The next investment is literally a financial investment in yourself. The two most powerful words on every doorstep to personal wealth are savings and compounding. Forget income; think net worth. Net worth is everything you own minus everything you owe. What's left is what will provide the funds for your retirement and the inheritance you plan for your children.

If you're not saving at least ten percent of household income and investing it wisely, you are spending a lot of money for a lot of crap. When you retire, that crap will be worthless and won't be able to sustain you in the lifestyle to which you are accustomed. You'll either have to change your lifestyle or work until you drop. There's a better way and it works. Remember, saving is easy, getting started is the hard part. Here's an example of a little saving and a reasonable amount of compounding. Do the math. How much will you have if you invest $2,000 per year for forty years, reinvest all returns and average a 12% return each year? My calculator says that adds up to $1,760,000. There's nothing magical about being a millionaire today. It takes savings and compounding. The more time you give it, the bigger the pot of gold at the end of your rainbow. The choices you make today determine whether you you can retire with peace of mind or be forced to work until your personal "D" day. Today's choices shape tomorrow's destiny.

The four biggest investments you can make are in yourself, in technology, in balance for your life and in investing in your future. For investments to work they need time to grow. Develop a written plan for each of these major areas and start working your plan. Success is no accident, and it shouldn't be a surprise, especially if you planned it. A regret is usually a result of a plan that wasn't conceived and acted on. Create your plan for a richer life.

Part III

Winning More Sales
By Acting Like A Pro

20. Improvisation: It ain't what it used to be

Which tools do you rely on to get the job done? Salespeople usually respond by listing their laptops, software, planners, pen, calculator, briefcase, FAX, pager, and digital telephone.

Here's another question: "What's the principle tool for all professional salespeople?" Guess! Guess again and even take another guess and I'll bet you can't guess right.

Let's take a brief detour to discover the principle tool for salespeople. Imagine you're a potter. Your products are hand-made and hand painted salt glaze pottery fired in your own kiln. If we asked a potter to describe his principle tool in making pots, he'd say it was his hands.

Without his hands there are no pots. They are absolutely essential in making clay pots. Other tools he relies on include a wheel, good clay, a kiln, water and a cutting knife for trimming the excess clay. To be successful he also needs a measure of talent.

Remember, the principle tool for a potter is his hands. Specifically, what then is the principle tool for salespeople? In all the times I've asked the question, no one has ever guessed. The most common responses I hear include personality, mind, creativity, communication skills, integrity, follow-up and others.

For me the answer is different and it's simple. The principle tool is just that, a tool. Use this tool wisely and you'll reach your selling destiny quicker. Without this tool, selling takes on a different dimension including fewer sales, longer selling cycles, less rapport with potential customers and if that's not enough, it will hit you where it hurts most, in your wallet.

I believe the principle tool for salespeople is words. Our thoughts are shaped with unspoken words. We use words to formulate our sales call objectives. Words are used to get appointments and build rapport. The questions we ask to uncover needs and problems are crafted with words. Throughout your presentation you'll rely on more words to handle objections as they arise. Finally, when the time is right, you'll secure the initial commitment, with words carefully prepared and practiced.

The language we use to sell with, consists of words that are chiseled out of our mental dictionaries. To know in advance which words you'll use in a given situation, creates a competitive advantage over salespeople who don't.

21. Practice: Like the millionaire next door

This is not about the book with the same name on the current best seller's list. This is about a regular guy who happened to win a million dollars.

Here's the story. I didn't see it happen because I was on a plane to San Diego. The story appeared in a *USA Today* article in the sports section. I read about it the day after the Pro Bowl game.

It happened during half-time. Dennis Crawford, a home improvement store manager, from Cleveland, Tennessee, kicked a perfect thirty-five yard field goal to win Hershey's Million Dollar Kick Challenge.

He won the Million Dollar prize. He was one of 518,000 entrants. He was one of four randomly chosen contestants. He beat the other three and earned the right to kick it through the uprights for the million dollars. Luck, right? He was just lucky, you're thinking. Well, up to the point his name was first selected, it was either luck or divine intervention. I'll concede luck.

"I practiced until my legs were sore." That was his response to reporters after winning. It had nothing to do with luck. He prepared, practiced and got the job done.

And how lucky must you be to succeed in selling? Imagine how much better your results would be if you prepared and practiced the primary selling skills. You would increase your competence and boost your confidence at the same time.

I prepare the words I want to use to make appointments. I rehearse them into a tape recorder. Once I have it down, I play the final tape over and over while I drive from account to account. "I practiced until my legs were sore."

When it comes to meeting potential customers for the first time, I develop my approach word for word. I rehearse into a tape recorder. Once I have it down, I play the final tape over and over while I drive from account to account. "I practiced until my legs were sore."

I realize how important questions are to understanding client needs. I prepared twelve questions, word for word until they are perfect. I rehearse into a tape recorder. Once I have it down, I play the final tape over and over while I drive from account to account. "I practiced until my legs were sore."

I know it's important to be able to ask for the order. I prepared exactly how I would ask. I rehearse into a tape recorder. Once I had it down, I played the final tape over and over while I drove from account to account. "I practiced until my legs were sore."

Success isn't limited to luck, though it may be a factor. It's about methodical preparation and regular practice. Why should you be living to the millionaire next door. Wouldn't you like it better if your neighbor was?

22. Instinct, impulse, and intuition: The antitheses to preparation

The sales representative who doesn't prepare key elements of the sales call in writing is forced to rely exclusively on his instincts. Your instincts, however, won't differentiate you from your competition, whereas your words will. All species known to mankind, share common instincts. Birds of the same species will mate at the same time. They'll build nests and care for their young chicks the same way. When it's time for the little ones to learn how to fly, I'll bet the flight instructors use similar flight plans.

It's the same with humans. Here are two examples. It's Saturday evening and you've just been seated at a fine restaurant. You are given menus, your cocktail order is taken. Drinks are served, dinner orders are taken, and in due time your meal is served. So far so good. What happens next, happens all the time. You will experience the same thing all over North America. It will happen in Toronto, New York, Chicago, Memphis, Sarasota, Houston, Albuquerque, San Diego, Portland and even in Sioux Falls.

Most waiters earn most of their money from tips. They want to make certain everything is okay. At some point during the meal, usually just after you put food into your mouth, your server will hover around your table and ask one of two questions. They will ask, "How is everything?," or ask "Is everything okay?" Consider this, no matter where you dine you will be asked one of those questions. Pure instinct is the reason. Those waiters weren't trained to ask those questions, they originated from instinct.

Here's another example. It's a beautiful Saturday morning. You closed a big sale during the week, and you plan to do some serious shopping as your reward. You enter the clothing section of your favorite department store. The retail clerk is doing a department scan and visually locks onto you. You know the feeling. You keep moving and so does he. He approaches closer and closer. What follows is a brief encounter, a stirring moment of professionalism, as he begins to speak and asks "Can I help you?" Overwhelmed by the magnitude of his words, you reply, "No thanks, I'm just looking." So I exaggerated a little. You get the point. Instinctively, if someone is going to offer help, the easiest way to ask is, "Can I help you?"

The waiter and the retail sales clerk committed the cardinal sin of selling. Neither prepared in advance. Both relied on their instincts. For them, the loss is minimal. If you rely on instinct, the potential loss is huge. Most elements of the selling process are routine, customary and repetitious. You do the same things over and over.

If it's going to be routine, why not make it a great and masterful routine. Follow these three steps for everything that's "routine" in selling. First, prepare it in writing in advance. Second, practice what you prepared to master it. Third, once you know the words, you can concentrate on the delivery. These are the repetitive elements to most selling situations.

Apply these steps to the following elements and your sales will take off.

1. Making appointments by telephone.

2. Building rapport and establishing credibility during the first sales call.

3. Asking twelve core questions to uncover specific needs and problems.

4. Presenting and positioning your product as a viable solution to these problems.

5. Handling concerns that become distractions.

6. Asking for the order.

This is what you do every day. Isn't there a better way?

Wouldn't you like to perform these tasks in a very professional way?

Wouldn't you want your potential customer to view you as a professional throughout the selling process?

Wouldn't you want to differentiate yourself from all your competitors?

Wouldn't you want to make more sales, more quickly, and earn more money?

If you answered "yes" to these questions, don't rely exclusively on your instincts. If you want to be better than your competitors, you must first be different. Become a wordsmith. Become a master wordsmith. Recognize the power of words. Appreciate the subtle difference between your choice of key words. There's a huge difference between lightning and the lightning bug.

Use power words often. Learn to speak in the active voice instead of the passive one. Prepare your key words in writing. Practice them often. In sales, your ultimate resource is words. Buy a notebook. Whenever you see a power word, write it down. Here's a short list of power words to get you started.

accomplish	achieve
build	create
direct	dominate
excel	execute
gain	increase
initiate	master
maximize	optimize
produce	reach
recognize	trigger

To summarize, instincts alone are for the birds. If you want to make a difference in selling more products to your potential customers, learn to use key words and power phrases. The right words, used to create power phrases will distinguish you from your unprepared competitors, who continue to "shoot from their lips" and "get mugged by their own mouths."

23. Preparation: Practice still makes perfect

The word preparation is a powerful one. It has many meanings including: "fitting, making ready, rehearsing, putting in order, building, foreseeing, developing, arranging, adapting, and adjusting." It's truly challenging to be prepared for the many and various scenarios that may occur during a sales call. When I think of preparation, I think of putting something in writing. When you organize your thoughts on paper, your preparation has begun and a plan is a likely outcome. It goes like this. Think it, write it, and do it. The person most prepared feels the least anxiety.

Be prepared - to have priorities. Priorities keep you organized and headed in the right direction. Schedule your priorities daily and you'll make better use of your time. Prioritize your accounts to optimize your call schedule. Your list is prioritized, if every item is numbered. If it isn't numbered, it isn't prioritized.

Be prepared - to set performance objectives. To achieve more results, carefully plan your objectives. Push yourself to go beyond the traditional sales and profit objectives which are predetermined for you by your company. What are the critical measurements to your success? Once they are identified, you can establish personal performance objectives and action plans to keep you on track.

Be prepared - to deal with a variety of people inside and outside of your company. Treat everyone with respect. Any time someone helps you give them an "Oscar." An "Oscar" is any word or deed that shows recognition, appreciation or gratitude. A thoughtful gesture goes a long way in today's rat-race world. People are starving for recognition, it doesn't cost much. Be a master delegator. The ultimate sign of trust is to ask someone to do something that you know you can do better. Delegating will free up lots of your time and telegraph to people that you trust them with the important stuff. Doing it yourself is not a good strategy. It may even limit your potential to achieve success.

Be prepared - to interact with different personalities. The dominant types (18%) are very direct in their approach. They are brief and to the point and want to focus on the task at hand. The expressives (28%) enjoy interaction with people. They want to socialize and give you their opinions. The amiables (40%) seek harmony and structure. They are very patient and expect a logical approach to the facts. The analytical types (14%) want data and facts. They are precise and accurate. They expect you to be very thorough. You can't take the "one size fits all" approach with everyone. To be effective you have to be adaptive. Become a student of what makes people tick and your sales will increase dramatically. If you want your sales to take off, adapt your style to to the customer's style.

Be prepared - to be passionate. Don't expect your potential customers to get excited about you and your products if you aren't. Today, there is so much busy-ness, that few people genuinely show their enthusiasm for the work. There's only one thing more contagious than the common cold and it's enthusiasm. Learn to get excited and stay excited about your work. The shortcut to passion begins with a smile. Passionate people are always smiling. Lets see some teeth on your next sales call.

Be prepared - to be persuasive. Persuasiveness contributes to successful selling if it's timed properly. Nothing turns a prospect off quicker than a persuasive sales person at the beginning of the selling process. Employ your ears before you engage your mouth. Persuasiveness should kick in only after you've completed your homework. Passionate persuasion can work miracles. Remember, not too much and never too early.

> *The more you know, the more you will have.*
> *Chinese Proberb*

> *In life, as in football, you won't go far unless you know where the goal posts are.*
> *Anonymous*

24. Telephones: The good, bad, and the ugly

The telephone can be a terrific business tool if used properly. As a professional sales representative in the 1970's I remember using the little red telephone booths scattered throughout the New York Thruway. Today's professional is likely to have a private line into his home office. He probably has a car phone and if he's a regular techno maven, he'll have a small digital phone for his briefcase or jacket pocket.

My problem was finding a phone. Your problem is finding the person you're calling. It's ironic, with the proliferation of telephones how tough it's become to reach someone on the first call. The rest of this chapter will focus on the problems you'll encounter when using the phone and how the telephone can be used to grow your business. Finally, I'll share four ideas that will enable you optimize your telephone results.

What doesn't work -

1. Busy signals - More people are spending more time on the phone, making it more difficult to get through. I guess that's why the recall button was invented.

2. Call waiting - How is it possible that something as convenient as call waiting, "you'll never miss another important call," can be so aggravating at the same time. You can deactivate call waiting

before making important calls and when you receive an important call. You can also ignore the call waiting signal which always says "you're more important" to the person you're talking to.

3. Area codes - If the number you're calling is older than six months, you can be out of luck. I'm on my third area code in six years. If you're worried about having to change your number again, invest in a toll free number. It's yours for life. And it can also save you some time and money in not having to reprint letterhead, envelopes, business forms, etc. Also call toll free information, 800-555-1212, to reach businesses who opted for 800 numbers after being forced to change area codes numerous times. You can also refer to "switchboard.com" to locate listings throughout the world.

4. Voice mail greetings - Some of these greetings have too many options and make it difficult to impossible to leave a quick message. Try dialing "0" or "1" to find a shortcut or even a real person.

5. Call forwarding - A great idea for the person who wants to continue to receive calls even when he changes locations. It's a bad idea however, if you're the caller and the person you're trying to reach, who has his calls forwarded, doesn't have the phone switched on or is temporarily away from his car. Technology is great, but don't let it outsmart you. Don't forward all calls. If you're expecting a call from someone important, give him your phone numbers and the approximate times you can be reached at each number. Everyone else

can wait. Proactive salespeople don't react to all calls in the same way.

6. Out of order, out of range, and out of FAX paper - If you want to win more sales, focus on being in touch not out of touch with your customers and prospective customers. There are no excuses for being out of anything, unless you're out of your mind. Stay on top of your telecommunications program to minimize the outages.

What works -

Here are some ideas on how to pro-actively use the telephone.

1. To call - Use your telephone to call someone especially if it can save you travel time that can be put to better use.

2. To confirm - Use your telephone to confirm meetings, understanding of a point, details of an order, a shipping schedule, or a back-order release. When you confirm something you are securing agreement on mutual understanding. It beats mayhem and confusion.

3. To congratulate - Use your telephone to give out those little "Oscars" to recognize people who have helped you in a special way. The phone can be used to wish someone a happy birthday, happy anniversary or to express your best wishes for the birth of a child or a job promotion. Don't hold back. Your kind words will have special meaning

considering the quick pace most folks operate in today.

4. To change - Use your telephone to change a variety of things including, appointment times, meetings, delivery dates, inventory status, tee times, and restaurants reservations.

5. To connect - One of the biggest benefits you get from using the telephone is your ability to stay connected with key customers, externally and internally. Use the telephone while driving and or waiting, to keep in touch with people you haven't kept in touch with.

6. To cancel - The easiest and second most personal way to cancel something is to use the telephone. Before you call to cancel, be sure you have clearly thought about your reason for doing so. Changing your plans and even canceling them may cause considerable inconvenience for someone else. If that someone happens to be a customer, you want to give a clear and rational reason for the change.

7. To convince - Salespeople routinely depend on their persuasiveness to secure closure. Few people cozy up to an "in-your-face selling style." When you feel it's appropriate to turn up the persuasive burners, do it in a subtle way. Always focus on how the customer benefits by taking action today. Before you make the call, use pencil and paper to sketch out what you'll say. A prepared presentation always beats one that's improvised. Your customer knows the difference.

8. To coordinate - Lone Rangers never had to worry about coordination activities. They did everything themselves because they couldn't trust others to do the task. Today, complex products and services depend on the successful integration and coordination of supplier teams with customer teams. Lone Rangers can't survive in this environment, facilitators can. Make sure you have each team member's phone, voice-mail, FAX number and e-mail address to permit timely coordination whenever it's required.

The telephone is a great business tool. It can drive you crazy and drive your business. How you use it makes the difference. Here are four ideas to get more productivity from your telephone.

1. Always have a mirror next to your office phone. Before you take a call or make a call, always check to see if you're smiling. This is a little idea that gets big results.

2. Always outline your thoughts and words on paper before you make really important calls. Speaking from your notes is better than shooting from your lips.

3. Use dynamic words and power phrases. Create a list of 200 power words. Refer to it before making important calls. You'll sound more professional incorporating words like "achieve, create, build, execute, master, gain, produce, accomplish" plus 192 of your other power words, into your telephone presentation.

4. If you expect someone to return a voice mail, make sure you get his attention. You gotta be different to make people want to respond to your telephone requests. Use your imagination and be creative. For example, "I'm giving up the game of golf until I hear from you." Sure it's corny, but it gets a laugh and often triggers the callback.

Don't take your telephone for granted. It can make you a powerful professional or tie you up like a calf in a rodeo. One of the quickest ways to increase your sales is to master the art of networking using the telephone. How do you spell productivity? I spell it "t-e-l-e-p-h-o-n-e!"

25. Your Approach: First the customer then the product

Today I talked about the sales approach. Tonight I want to write about it. Today when I discussed the approach, it was a part of a three-day sales training program. After two days the class was tired. Most were anxious to go home. What could be easier than talking about your first sales call to a major account? What's more important than making a solid first impression during this call? They just didn't seem to get it.

The class was young. Sure they were eager to learn. They were also eager to hold onto to old habits and ancient ideas about selling. I was encouraging them to prepare and they wanted to be spontaneous. They wanted to wing the first call, you know play it by ear, "wait until I get there" was their way. I wanted their first sales call, at least one very important part of it to be scripted, practiced, memorized and delivered in a conversational way that would seem professional, competent and natural from the customer's perspective.

First I'd like to describe the approach element of an initial sales call. Usually when you meet someone for the first time, we do the "automatics." We automatically greet the person by shaking hands, briefly introducing our self and trying to establish some rapport. We automatically attempt to identify common interests and we automatically engage the customer in small talk or chit chat.

The generally stated purpose of most initial sales calls is to uncover specific customer needs. This is achieved by asking really good questions. So, you're wondering, if all this is true, what's the approach? The approach is how you bridge from the chit chat to your first question. It's your technique for getting down to business. It's as important as your first serve in a tennis match. It's more important than your drive on the first tee at your favorite golf course.

Salespeople are often too preoccupied on the first call to get the appointment for the second call. Securing the appointment for the second call before you leave is always a good idea. It's also a solid idea to make a really good first impression before you start planning the second sales call.

If you want to make an excellent transition from chit chat to your first question, follow these steps.

1. Forget winging it. To do this properly you'll need pencil and paper or fingers and a keyboard.

2. Think of your bridge as a bridge and transition from chit chat to your first question.

3. Choose power words you are very comfortable with.

4. These words are the preamble to your first question.

5. Remember, your approach signifies that you are getting down to business.

6. Your approach also tells your customer that you plan to start with questions, not with a sales presentation.

7. Count the words and eliminate unnecessary ones.

8. Once prepared, twice practiced and you'll have a polished approach.

Meeting a potential customer for the first time is no time to stumble and ramble. Lasting relationships begin with good first impressions. Improvisation is okay. Being prepared, practiced, and professional is even better.

What you do speaks so loudly, that I cannot hear what you say.
                                        Ralph Waldo Emerson

The secret of success is doing what you do well.
                                        Longfellow

26. Opportunities: The twelve best questions to ask potential customers

If you want to ask really good questions, you must do three things. First you must prepare them. Once prepared, they must be organized in a logical sequence. Finally, you must be sure to ask them.

The following are my favorite questions. Some aren't even stated as questions, but they work the same way - they get the customer talking. If you like them, please use them. If they don't quite fit your mouth, change them. These questions work for me, and I'm confident if you give them a try, they'll work for you.

1. Tell me about your business. It's a very broad request by design. What usually comes to the surface pretty quickly is what's important to the potential customer. If you're selling products to the government, you can substitute the word "organization" for the word "business." The beauty of a really good question is that it eliminates all assumptions. It forces you to start with your potential customer, not with your products.

2. Describe the people in your organization. Once again, it's a very broad question that's designed to get the potential customer talking about what's important to him. Listen carefully to his response to this one. You will be rewarded with how this

person feels about and possibly relates to other key people in his organization.

3. What are your responsibilities? Once you discover the role, title, or position within an organization also probe to find out what a person's responsibilities are. Here's where you'll get a view of his ego, self esteem and self worth. Most salespeople never ask this question because they make goofy assumptions based on what they know about certain jobs.

4. What are the biggest challenges you face in growing your business? This is a terrific question and the key word is "challenges." It's a positive word that uncovers negative stuff. As a professional salesperson, your job is to identify specific needs and problems. When you first meet a potential customer, it's not always easy for him to open up to a stranger about problems, regardless of your sincerity and willingness to help. To speed up the process, focus on challenges instead of problems. Most people are more than willing to describe their biggest challenges, while reluctant to tell you about their problems. Change the way you ask the question, and you'll see how they change the way they respond to you.

5. What are your priorities? A five word question. It doesn't get easier than this one and it's gem. Here's what you'll learn. Some people don't have priorities and this question makes those people easy to spot. If they do have priorities, they'll describe them in detail. If you get a long list, ask

the customer to prioritize it for you. If on the other hand, the list is small, ask the customer if there are any additional priorities. This is an assumption buster question. If you don't ask it, you are probably making too many assumptions about your potential customers. The response to this question paves the way for you to tailor your presentation to match the customer's priorities. Remember to take detailed notes after you ask this question.

6. Ask a relationship question. Of the twelve questions, this one may vary according to the situation. It's a personal question, designed to learn about common interests and things that contribute over time to building a personal relationship. Often you'll notice pictures, trophies, plaques and other memorabilia that reveal these personal interests. This is a relationship question. Ask any question that advances the relationship to a higher level.

7. What do you like most about your current supplier? Put your ego aside for this one. Naturally, you want to hear that he doesn't like anything about his current supplier and that's why he's agreed to speak with you. In the real world, however, he probably likes something about his present supplier. These are his hot buttons. It doesn't make a difference whether your products can deliver these hot buttons or not, you must know what they are before you begin your sales presentation.

8. If you could change anything about your current supplier, what would you change? This question is an exception to the ten word maximum. I just like it this way. It's a powerful question and if you are patient, you will be rewarded with a good response. Remember this; fifty percent of the time his first response will be, "I can't think of anything." Be patient and recognize that nothing is perfect. Ask the question again, and wait patiently for his answer. Remember, no one is ever 100% satisfied. What you're searching for is that dissatisfaction. Once identified, you have a starting point to build your presentation on. People are always looking to improve their current situation. Don't make any assumptions. This is the opportunity question.

9. What's your criteria for making a decision? I'm absolutely amazed at how infrequently this question is asked, especially since it's one of the most powerful questions in the line-up. You'll discover if your customer even has criteria. If he does, he'll tell you what they are. Once he describes the criteria, you can ask him to prioritize them for you. When he answers this questions he is telling you what he is going to specifically base his decision on. Ask one hundred different people and you'll hear one hundred different answers. How could you begin to make an intelligent sales presentation without knowing what his decision is going to be based on? Try this one on for size and you'll get an immediate payback.

10. Describe your decision making process. The criteria and process are related yet different. You need to know what criteria will be evaluated before the decision is made. You also want to know the process involved in making a decision. What steps will he actually go through to reach a final decision. Basically you'll learn whether it going to be a toss of the coin or a more complicated process. Either way, you'll be better positioned to tailor your presentation to accommodate his criteria and the process he'll use to make a decision.

11. How will you measure success when using our products? This is one of my favorite questions. It's so revealing it's scary. You will hear things that you couldn't have imagined in your wildest dreams. That's the beauty of the question. There's no way you can accurately anticipate a response to this question. Ask the question, relax, and listen carefully to the answers you get. This question unearths the personal and critical measurements the individual has for your product. Wouldn't you like to hear the answer to this one before you started to sell your products? You bet!

12. What are your expectations for working with a new supplier? This one is very straight forward. Expectations are a powerful and dominant influence. If you want to build a long-term customer relationship, ask the expectations question. If you think you already know . . . how could you possibly know if you haven't asked? That's the point. It's a great question. Try it and you'll be delighted with the results.

Jim Meisenheimer

There are so many reasons for asking really good questions and only one reason for not asking them. We don't ask really good questions if we're in a rush to make the sale. This isn't about making a sale, it's about building a relationship. It's about helping potential customers make more informed decisions. It's about professional salespeople doing their homework before selling their products. It's about getting to know your customers in order to fit your products to their specific needs. When that happens good things happen to your customers and even better things happen to you.

Always start with your questions before you present your solutions. If you listen to their words, they will buy from you.

27. Speaking: Make your stand-up presentations stand-out

Anybody can give a speech sitting down. The greatest conversationalist, perched on your family room sofa, might not be as comfortable or eloquent if he were asked to stand up and present his thoughts to all those in attendance. The same is true for professional salespeople. Some really shine during one-on-one presentations and others can't wait to get up on the platform.

Thirteen years ago I was Vice President of sales for the Scientific Products division of American Hospital Supply. In that role I often traveled to our regional offices to meet with our local sales representatives and customers. It was on one of those trips that I encountered a terrified Dave. Dave was our top west coast sales rep. Overall he ranked second in the country in gross profit dollar production. He was really good. What I liked most about Dave was his soft-sell approach. He was always quietly enthusiastic. But he was definitely enthusiastic. I had known Dave for several years.

On this particular day I was having lunch with Dave. It was the mid-day break during a joint regional sales meeting. That meant that two regions, each with twelve sales reps, were pooling their resources and a shared agenda to exchange ideas and learn new selling skills.

After I was two bites into my sandwich and taking a pull from my diet Pepsi, I noticed Dave was perspiring, really perspiring and he looked a little peaked. I asked him if he was feeling alright. With a slightly embarrassed expression on his face, he told me he was okay, but nervous and anxious about the twenty-minute presentation he was scheduled to give to his peers after lunch. I couldn't believe our number two guy, was that nervous about getting up in front of his co-workers. There he was though, gushing perspiration like a fire hydrant.

Later that night I thought about my own nervousness in front of groups. I remembered my senior year in high school. I was just elected student council president. The principal, Mr. Van Brunt, who looked a lot like the infamous Mr. Clean, told me that one of my new responsibilities during the next school year would be to go up on stage every time there was a student assembly and recite the pledge of allegiance. I spent most of my senior year worrying about those nerve shattering assemblies.

My fear of speaking didn't subside until my junior year of college. I'll never forget the experience. One day, about the fifth week into the semester of an R.O.T.C. class our instructor, Captain Dwyer looked and pointed at three student cadets. Yours truly was one of them. He barked out our names and said that each one of us was to present a chapter out of the text book for the next class.

Holy butterflies. I had to get up and teach a class and I had only two days to get ready. Well, I was so scared I prepared. I prepared so much I didn't have time to be nervous. All my energy was focused on the preparation. When I got up to give my presentation, the butterflies were still there, but I had them flying in a military formation.

Over the years, I've learned a few things about giving stand-up presentations. Here are six practical ideas to consider before you give your next group presentation.

1. Never begin a stand-up presentation with an improvised opening. Prepare and practice your first thirty to fifty words. Hit your audience right between the eyes. Use a quotation, a story, a rhetorical question or make a compelling statement. Your goal is to grab them and let them know this is going to be different and good.

2. Tell them what you're going to tell them. Be creative. Tap into their emotions. Remember, there are too many boring presentations being given every day. Do anything but don't be boring and bland.

3. Avoid too much detail. A really good presentation is a conversation with your audience. Don't present the details, write them down and hand them out. Talk about the key points. Pepper your speech or presentation with stories and anecdotes. People love personal experiences simply because most folks can relate to them.

4. Remember the first rule of successful presentations. You are the message. Not your overheads, not your slides and certainly not your fancy pancy Power Point presentations. They are aids and tools and if used properly make you look and sound better. Also remember the second rule. The second rule is never forget the first rule. Think of yourself as a billboard. Also think about what you want

yours to say. Be real and be alive. Whenever you present, you're either adding energy to the room or sucking oxygen out of it.

5. Watch your hands. If you're not accustomed to giving stand-up presentations to groups, your hands can be problematic. Your hands will migrate to your pockets, behind your back, and if your not careful even to the olive branch position with hands crossed. Use your hands to make key points. If you give them a chance your hands will make you animated.

6. Try to be yourself. I realize that may be bad advice for some people, but do your best to be authentic. You'll fare much better by being the real McCoy than trying to be a carbon copy of someone else. If no two people are exactly alike, why try to act like someone else. Develop your personal brand and style for doing things. Become a genuine, caring human being who doesn't put on airs and your presentations will always be well received. Authenticity, more than anything else, makes your stand-up presentations stand-out.

Anybody can give a speech sitting down. The next time you're preparing for a group presentation, review these six guidelines. Your next stand-up presentation will stand-out if you do.

28. Objections: How to get fewer ones and how to handle the ones you get

"Where do I sign?" That's what you'd like to hear on every sales call. Unfortunately, it doesn't always happen that way. What does happen is you routinely meet with customer resistance. You can't make it disappear, but you can delay it and learn how to handle it more effectively when it does occur.

There are three points to this chapter. First: When do you typically get objections? How early in the sales call? If you're selling professionally you shouldn't hear objections early in the selling process. Second: How do you classify the objections? Which ones do you keep hearing over and over again? Recurring objections are gifts. You can prepare for them. Third. I'll show you how to deal with objections you do get, practically and professionally.

Early in the sales call, your goal is to discover customer needs. You do that by asking really good questions. You want to employ your ears before you engage your mouth. Your ears will out earn your mouth every day in the week. Potential customers usually express needs when they are talking, not when you are talking - get the point. Hearing objections rather than needs early in the sales call is a good indicator the wrong person is doing most of the talking.

Jim Meisenheimer

Here are the generic and typical steps salespeople must navigate to secure the purchase order. It may vary slightly for your business.

1. Establish rapport and build credibility.

2. Discover customer's specific needs and problems.

3. Present and position your product as the tailored solution to your customer's situation and specific problems.

4. Handle concerns as they come up.

5. Secure the commitment.

The selling road is filled with objections, however, you shouldn't get them at the first turn. The easiest way to avoid getting bogged down with early objections is to ask really good questions. Your questions should be open and expansive. It's during this part of the sales call you should let your curiosity hang out. Consider yourself an ace at asking questions, when you can recite ten open-ended questions without blinking, hesitating, and using any ""um's" and "ah's"." Here are ten questions to get you started. These questions and others you prepare in advance will help you to sell more and earn more and do it in less time. This is added reinforcement to an earlier chapter.

1. Tell me about your business.

2. What are your responsibilities?

3. In addition to yourself, who else is involved with this project?

4. What are the biggest challenges you face?

5. What are your priorities for this project?

6. What do you like most about your current supplier?

7. If you could change anything about your current product, what would it be?

8. What qualities are you looking for in a supplier?

9. What's your criteria for making a decision?

10. How do you measure success in working with your current supplier?

Your road to success should be paved with really good questions that you know like the back of your hand.

If you know how to avoid objections early in the sales call, what happens when you get them later? First, what kind of objections are you getting? How often are you getting them? Have you written them down, word for word? Do you know exactly what you say prior to you hearing the objection? You could inadvertently be triggering the objections. Do your homework and answer these questions in writing.

Identify the two most common and frequently heard objections you get. Write them down - word for word exactly as you hear them. Then say, "thank you." These are gifts. By definition a recurring objection happens over and over again. You will get this objection next week and the week after. Never again should you act surprised when you hear a recurring objection. Instead, prepare and practice what you will say the next time you hear it. You can't prepare for the objection you never heard before. You can prepare for the one you know you'll hear next week.

If you take this advice two things will happen. First, whenever you hear the objection your chin will be up in the locked and confident position. Second, and it's linked to the first, you will hear the objection less frequently. I used to get the "your fee is too high" objection all the time. Now, because I know exactly - word for word, how I'll respond to it, I don't hear it as often. I still get it, just not as often. When I hear the price objection - I deal with it confidently and directly. Bingo!

All objections known to mankind can be classified into four basic types. No money, no hurry, no need, and no confidence. When you hear money you must emphasize value. When there's no hurry, create a sense of urgency. When's there's no need, keep asking questions to uncover one. When you hear no confidence, show them the customer testimonials. Every proposal I send out includes a stack of fifty very recent customer testimonials in the form of letters, cards or e-mails.

Now to the fun stuff. How should you handle and respond to recurring objections? What is an objection? In Webster's *New World Thesaurus*, the synonyms for the word objection include: "disapproval, hesitation, question, demurring, reluctance, disinclination, unwillingness, rejection, dislike, dissatisfaction, discontent, displeasure, repugnance, disesteem, disapprobation, shrinking, boggling, shunning, revulsion, repudiation, low opinion, abhorrence, unacceptance, discarding, dubiousness, and doubt." No wonder you're so intimidated by them.

Actually an objection is seldom that severe in nature. It could mean other things as well. A "no" could mean: not yet, not now, maybe, I need more information, you have to add more value, I need more time, or it depends.

It could mean almost anything but an absolutely, positively, without a doubt resounding NO.

When you hear an objection what should you do with it? Simple. Spin it around. A circle has 365 degrees. Draw a large circle on a sheet of paper. On the top of the page write (word for word) a recurring objection. For the purpose of this exercise, assume you've written "can you do any better on your price," on the top of the page. Now go to the circle and place a tick mark anywhere on the northern part of the circle. Imagine that tick mark represents the objection. It takes up one degree. What would happen to the intensity of the objection, if you could move someone 90 degrees away from their original point or 180 degrees? It would become less intense and not as important.

You can't vaporize objections. You can and should attempt to soften, dissolve, mellow, lessen, thaw, diminish, melt, moderate, bend, relax, weaken, modify, tone down, and tenderize them. For example, the price objection. I suspect you have to deal with that one occasionally. Using the circle and thinking creatively, identify all the issues related to price. High price, low price, high quality, low quality, reliability, applications, credibility, maintenance, adaptability, large company, small company, new company, veteran company. This requires outside-the-box thinking. It's grunt work. You can't do this fast and furious. Think about opposites, counter points, reverses, inverses, extremes, contradictions etc.

Put your thoughts on paper. Actually what hits the paper are words. The words develop into phrases and ultimately into a professional response to a recurring objection. You want to put a spin on the recurring objection. It should be logical and well thought out. You can't ever do this as well when you're improvising.

Here are some phrases that have worked with some of my clients. They are partial statements used to handle a variety of objections. Read them slowly. Their intent is to force the listener to consider other view points - moving the potential customer away from the original objection.

> How do you think our company got to be 118 years old?

> Do you think if our competitor could get our prices, they wouldn't try?

> We know our price is high, and there is a reason.

> If the lower priced product failed, what would your total cost then be?

> Our price may be higher but our total cost is lower.

Your response to a recurring objection should never be given in an off-the-cuff manner. I can't possibly give you universal responses to objections. You have to do your homework. Let me summarize the steps to preparing professional prepared responses to recurring objections.

1. Identify two recurring objections.

2. Write them down verbatim the way you hear them.

3. Write down the words you generally use that triggers these objections.

4. Draw a circle with the objection written on the top of the page.

5. Identify the issues that circle the objection. Write key words all over the circle.

6. Do step five over at least three times on different days.

7. Play with the words and convert them into power phrases.

8. Once your response is honed and polished, practice it until it is anchored.

I'm asking you do something you probably have never done before. That's why is so important for you to do it. You'll meet with less resistance from your potential customers. You'll get more business and get it more quickly. You'll gain poise during tough situations. You'll beat the brains out of your competition because they won't take the time to do it. If you do it you'll win more sales, if you don't you won't.

Jim Meisenheimer

The road to selling is filled with detours and potholes. Put your smart suit on and determine what's in your way (objections) and figure out a way around it. Henry Ford said it best, when he said, "Don't complain, don't explain. Just deal with it."

Stupidity is the deliberate cultivation of ignorance.
William Gaddis

Learning teaches more in one year than experience in twenty.
Roger Ascham

You write a hit play the same way you write a flop.
William Saroyan

29. Value Statements: Learn how to create value to avoid the fatal flaw in selling

How would you like to win every sales opportunity that you work on? It would be nice work if you could arrange it. How would you like to lose every sales opportunity that you work on? No doubt, you'd like to take a pass on that one. While neither scenario is likely, there is one quality that separates the two extremes. It's the quality of preparation. Let me give you an example.

Last June I stayed at the Vancouver Hyatt for four days. I was there for a Canadian Management Seminar on sales management. Most of my trips are shorter ones and when I'm scheduled to be away that long I'll often try to buy a small gift for Bernadette, my wife.

There was an underground mall beneath the Hyatt. On the evening of the second day of the seminar, I decided to go for a walk and while stretching my legs, see if I could find an appropriate gift for Bernadette. One small shop caught my eye. It was a specialty shop that sold jewelry made from a variety of gems and minerals. Naturally I was more interested in the minerals.

I walked into the store and did my ninety second browse and search tour. The shop seemed to have a number of nice and reasonably priced pieces that I was looking for. The shopkeeper saw me and said, "hello." I returned the greeting and left soon after.

The next night I returned. I had a plan. I had identified two pieces of jewelry that I thought Bernadette would like. Before entering the store, I thought about my approach and the amount of money I wanted to spend. I also thought about the specific words I'd use.

I walked directly over to the shopkeeper. I said, "I need to get my wife a gift tonight." He told me to look around and call him if I needed assistance. I spotted the necklace and earrings I wanted. They were malachite, a green marble like mineral. The price was $125 Canadian. I waved for the shopkeeper. He came right over.

I asked him, "How much better can you do on the price?"

He reached for his calculator, punched in a few numbers and said he could give me a 14% discount.

Looking straight down at the jewelry, I sighed, "That's more than I wanted to spend." I remained silent, and once again he punched more numbers into his calculator.

Finally he looked up and said, "I'll give you 20% off." I bought the necklace and earrings and got the discount as a bonus. I was ready to pay list price. He didn't ask, so he didn't know.

His strategy was to talk price. It should have been to show me the value. I was prepared and he wasn't - the fatal flaw in selling.

30. Closing: Forget closing, it's about opening

Several years ago PBS Television invited me to speak to their station affiliates. Each station is responsible for fund raising and program sponsorships. While it's not like making a traditional sale, there is a beginning and an end to the process. The end, or commitment, is commonly referred to as closing, much the same way most salespeople refer to it.

PBS asked me to do a one hour session called "Closing The Sale." As a sales trainer, I had spoken many times on the subject of closing, however this was the first time anyone asked me to speak exclusively on this subject. I decided to do some homework. The first thing I did was look up the word in a dictionary. What a surprise! It wasn't defined exactly the way I anticipated. According to the dictionary, "to close" meant to "liquidate, neutralize, and eradicate," among other things.

If closing comes at the end of the selling cycle, it really signals the beginning or opening of the account, not the closing of it, and certainly not its eradication. Personally, I feel some salespeople fail to "close" the sale because they don't find it easy to do. With few exceptions it's hard to say that closing is a positive experience.

Let's reframe it and call it something else. Instead of closing, how about securing commitment or asking for the order or getting the decision. These are more positive and accurate descriptors of what actually happens at the end of the selling cycle.

Enough theory. Here are several ways to help someone say yes or no. Naturally we're looking for yes's. We don't want maybe's. If all the maybe's salespeople had were cashed in tomorrow, we would have enough to eliminate the national debt. Real winners don't bank on maybe's, they're searching for the yes's.

Here are a few simple yet effective ways to ask for the order. You should only use these statements after all potential customer needs have been identified, your solutions have been presented, and after all major concerns have been effectively handled. Once you're in this position consider one of these.

> Do you have enough information to make a decision or would you prefer a demonstration?
>
> What would you like the next step to be?
>
> If you don't have any questions, I'll go ahead and write up the order?
>
> We can provide the technical product training at your location or at our corporate training center, which would be better for your technician?
>
> You seem very positive about our proposal, why don't we take the next step to schedule the delivery.

Do you have any questions or would you like
to take the next step?

Think of all the reasons you put off "closing the sale." If you ever get anxious about securing the commitment in the future take this advice. Decide how you will ask for the order before you make the sales call. Since it will be brief, write it down. Count the words, once you feel comfortable with your approach, practice it at least twelve times. Your total time investment will be less than a minute. The return on your investment will be an incredible boost to your confidence. Everything gets easier with practice. Put yourself in your customer's shoes for a moment. It's easier to say no to someone who is winging it. It's more difficult to say no to a professional. Bringing closure to the selling cycle, is no time for improvisation.

It pays to prepare. It pays more to practice. It pays even more to prepare and practice often. If you want to be paid more, do what pays more.

FREE! Special Selling Report #3 with all orders over $100 **FREE!**
You'll also get the NEW & FREE biweekly
Sales Strategist Updates via e-mail

FAX ORDER FORM (FAX 941-907-0441)

Item	Unit	No.	Total
Books			
12 Best Questions To Ask Custome	$19.95		
57 Ways To Take Control Of Your Time And Your Life	$19.95		
CD's			
How To Get Surefire selling Results	$199.00		
How to Sell Anything For List Price	$57.00		
35 Ways To Differentiat Yourself From Competitors	$57.00		
How To Adapt Your Selling Style	$37.00		
How To Get Spectacular Results In The 4th Quarter	$37.00		
Closing the Sale	$37.00		
		Subtotal	
Tax (IL residents add 6.5%)			
Shipping & handling ($2/tape, $2/book, $.50/selling report)			
		TOTAL	

See reverse side for billing information

Please call for special value pricing when ordering large quantities.

Method of Payment:

_____ Check or Money Order (make payable to JM Associates)

_____ Visa   Acct. #_____   Exp. Date_____

_____ Master   Acct. #_____   Exp. Date_____
        Card

Customer Information:

Name   _____

Company Name   _____

Address   _____

City/State/Zip Code   _____

Phone/FAX   _____

e-mail Address   _____

Purchase Order #   _____

Jim Meisenheimer, Inc.

Sales Strategist
13506 Blythefield Terrace
Lakewood Terrace, FL 34202

Phone   **FAX**
800.266.1268   941.907.0441

Web site   **email**
www.meisenheimer.com   jim@meisenheimer.com

Resources

Selling Power
800-752-7355

Success
800-234-7324

DISC - Personal Insights Profile
800-266-1268

Sales & Marketing Management
800-821-6897

Telephone Selling Report
402-895-9399

Nightingale-Conant Audio Tapes
800-525-9000